W9-CKE-417

Sunset Travel Guide to
ALASKA

By the Editors of
Sunset Books and
Sunset Magazine

Lane Publishing Co.
Menlo Park, California

Edited by Barbara J. Braasch

Hours, admission fees, prices, telephone numbers, and highway designations in this book are accurate as of June 1978.

Maps have been provided in each chapter for the special purpose of highlighting significant regions, routes, or attractions in the area. Check automobile clubs, insurance agencies, the state tourist office, or travel agents as possible sources for detailed road maps of Alaska.

Thanks...

to the many people and organizations who assisted in the preparation of this travel guide. Special appreciation goes to Bill and Sally Bishop, Heida Boucher, D. A. Brady, Bob Giersdorf, Julie Anne Gold, Richard Montague, Jack Musiel, Anne Shrum, and Suzy Warton who gave invaluable help in compiling and verifying information.

Design: Cynthia Hanson
Artwork and maps: Ted Martine

Cover: Waterside view of Ketchikan in Southeast Alaska. Photographed by Paul Chan.

Editor, Sunset Books: David E. Clark

Fourth printing March 1983

Copyright © 1978, 1966, 1963, Lane Publishing Co., Menlo Park, CA 94025. Third edition. World rights reserved. No part of this publication may be reproduced by any mechanical, photographic, or electronic process, or in the form of a phonographic recording, nor may it be stored in a retrieval system, transmitted, or otherwise copied for public or private use without prior written permission from the publisher. Library of Congress Catalog Card Number: 77-90724. ISBN 0-376-06035-2. Lithographed in the United States.

Contents

Introduction to a great land

Alaska stretches spatial concepts. It is a land of superlatives and impressive statistics. Encompassing four time zones (Pacific, Yukon, Alaska, and Bering) and 586,400 square miles, the 49th state is roughly as large as California, Arizona, Nevada, Oregon, and Washington put together, with land enough left over to form South Carolina.

Among its scenic splendors are Mt. McKinley, highest peak in North America; 5,000 glaciers, one larger than Switzerland; 3 million fresh water lakes, one qualifying as America's second largest; and a farming community where it is not uncommon to find cabbages weighing more than 70 pounds.

Yet this vast area is thinly populated. Around half of the state's over 400,000 residents live in one metropolitan area, Anchorage. Three-quarters of the remainder reside in a half dozen cities. The rest are scattered around the state in some 250 tiny villages.

Original native Alaskans probably migrated from Asia over a then-existing land bridge between Asia and North America. Some early settlers may have sledded over the frozen Bering Strait or paddled skin boats across the water in summertime.

Today's native population numbers about 60,000, divided into three major groups: Aleuts, Eskimos, and Indians. Eskimos, the largest group, clustered around the Arctic coastline. The Indians migrated into the interior, following the caribou. Though Athabascan Indians still live in the interior, the Tlingit, Haida, and Tsimshian Indians shifted down into Southeastern Alaska.

(Continued on page 8)

Massive *Mendenhall Glacier's cracked, ice-blue face lies a short distance north of Juneau.*

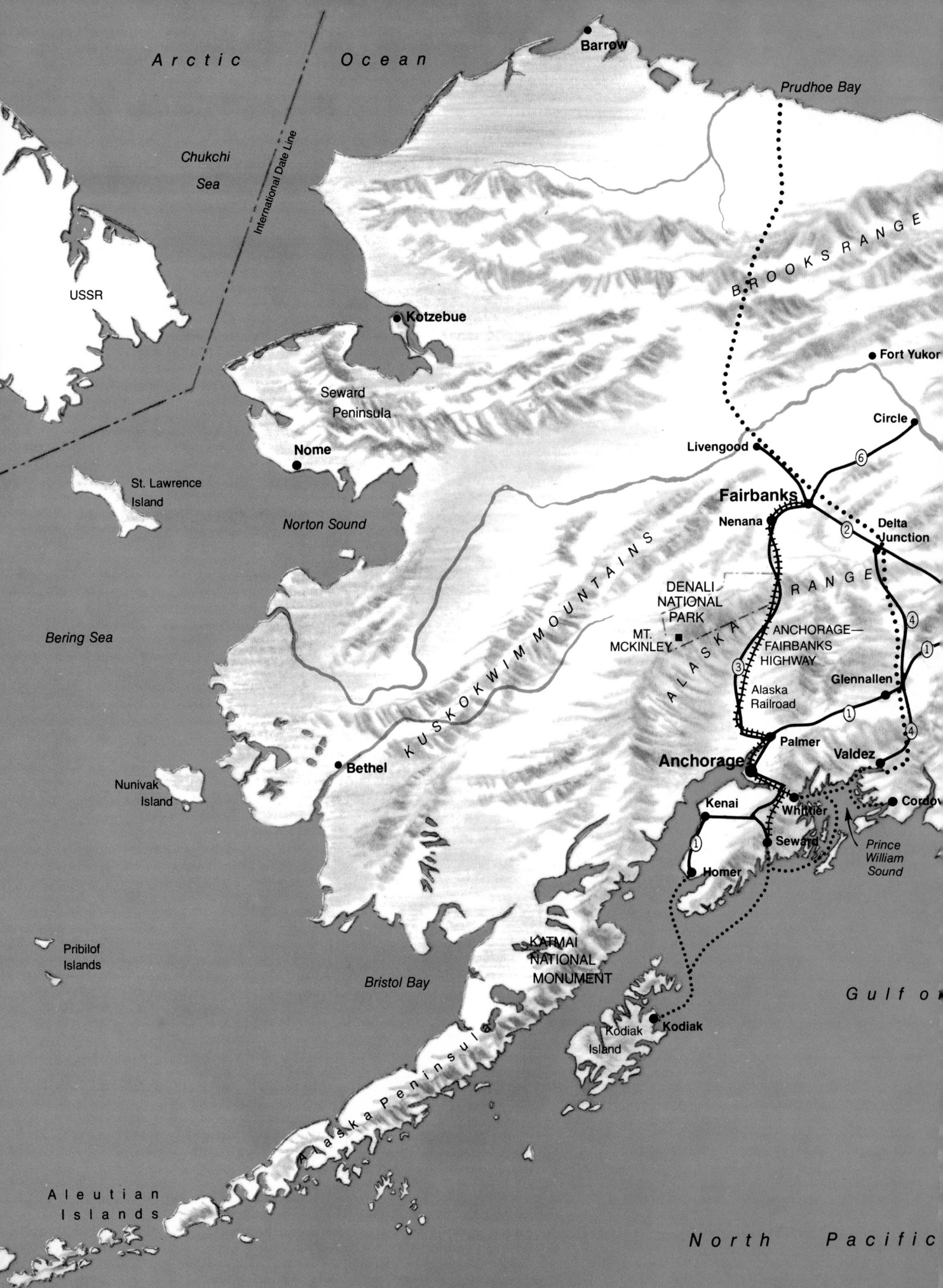

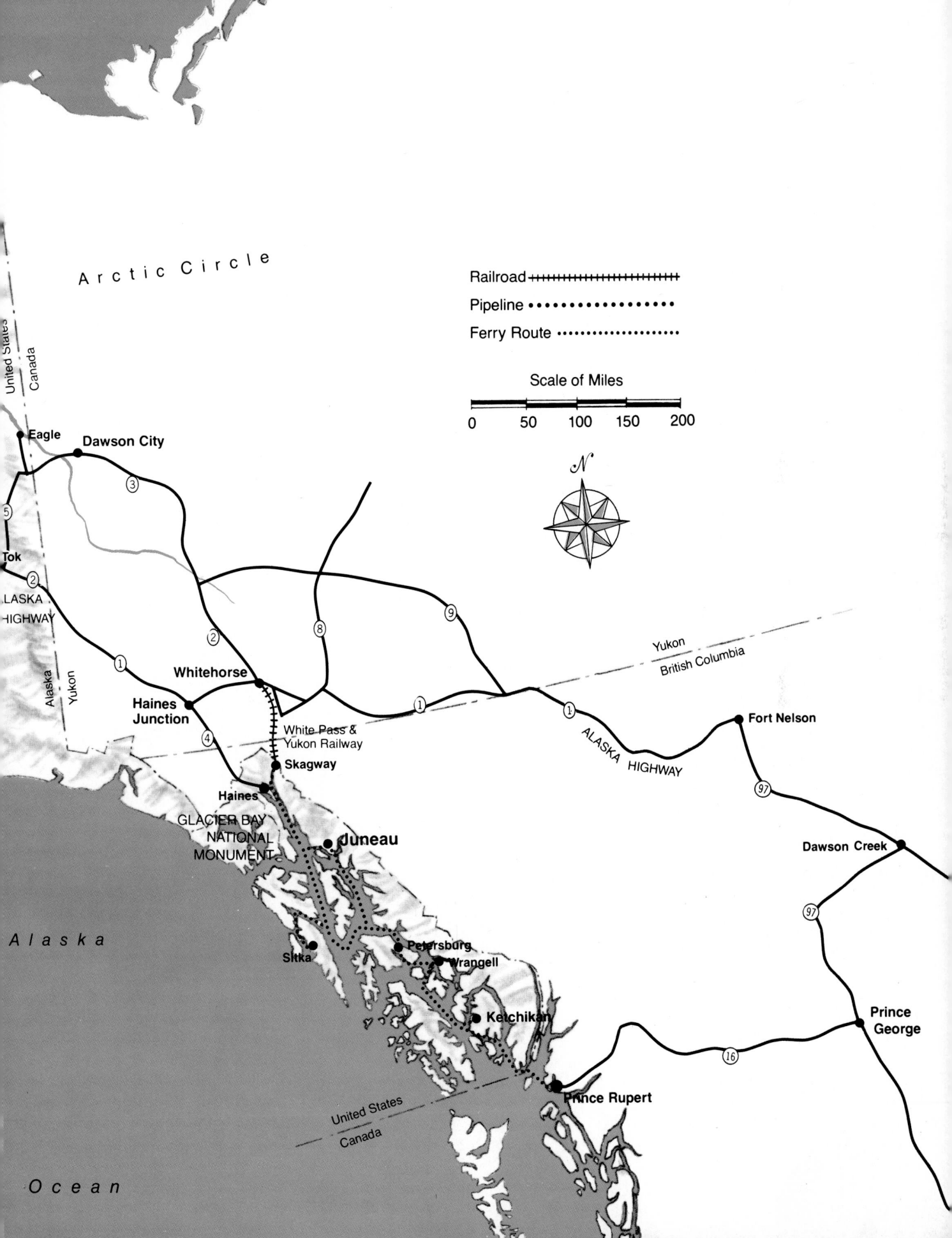

Railroad ++++++++++++++++++
Pipeline ••••••••••••••••••
Ferry Route •••••••••••••••

Scale of Miles

0   50   100   150   200

Arctic Circle

United States
Canada

Eagle   Dawson City

③

⑤

Tok

②

ALASKA
HIGHWAY

Alaska

Yukon

①

Whitehorse

Haines
Junction

④

②

⑧

⑨

Yukon
British Columbia

①

①

ALASKA
HIGHWAY

Fort Nelson

⑨⑦

White Pass &
Yukon Railway

Skagway

Haines

GLACIER BAY
NATIONAL
MONUMENT

Juneau

Dawson Creek

⑨⑦

Alaska

Sitka

Petersburg
Wrangell

Ketchikan

Prince
George

United States
Canada

Prince Rupert

⑯

Ocean

...Continued from page 5

Aleuts—adept seamen that they were—settled along the islands named for them and around the southwestern corner of Alaska.

Geography on a large scale

Alaska comes from an Aleut word, *Alyeska*, meaning "great land." And great it is. No matter how you travel, the geological book of nature is there to read.

Ice-age sculptured mountains still wear frozen caps, and glacial fingers poke down deep canyons. Southeast's famed Inside Passage was carved out as a result of ice-cutting and melting. Meandering rivers—the Yukon, Kuskokwim, Copper, Taku, Stikine, and others—sliced tremendous valleys along their courses. Mountain ranges loom as colossal, ragged wrinkles on the landscape.

At times, molten magma breaks out from beneath the earth's crust, forming volcanoes and spewing wide lava flows. Everywhere, dramatic landscapes dwarf the viewer.

Geographically, you'll discover five distinct Alaskas: Southeastern, Gulf Coast, Western, Interior, and Arctic. Separated from British Columbia by the crest of the Coastal Range, Southeast Alaska extends from Haines and Skagway in the north to Ketchikan in the south. The Gulf Area includes the region north and west of Haines, around the Gulf of Alaska. Western Alaska includes the Alaska Peninsula and the Aleutian and Pribilof islands.

Interior Alaska, located north of the Alaska Range, sprawls from the Canadian border. It takes in the headwaters of the Copper, Yukon, Kuskokwim, and Tanana waters; edges along the Arctic Circle; and spreads to the Bering Sea. North and west to the Yukon River and the shores of the Arctic Ocean, Arctic Alaska includes endless tundra lands, rolling treeless hills, and the jagged Brooks Range south of the Arctic slope.

Ceremonial house *mesmerizes visitor at Totem Bight Park in Ketchikan.*

Still a frontier adventure?

Civilization has encroached slowly on Alaska's vast expanse. Because towns are few and far between, much of the large state retains its pristine quality.

Visitors to the 49th state may feel as if the clock stopped about a hundred years ago. Terrain and climate have preserved some of the frontier conditions that have long since vanished in the "Lower 48." In many places you'll still find boardwalks, false front buildings, and unpaved streets. Although Anchorage appears quite cosmopolitan, its modern veneer is thin. Fairbanks may remind you of a boom town that grew too rapidly for careful planning.

Planning for the future is, in fact, one of Alaska's biggest headaches. Oil and gas exploration in the Arctic and on the Kenai Peninsula has replaced the more glamorous gold and fur trade. Fishing and lumbering businesses are expand-

ing, despite a battle raging between commercial interests in land development and those people who would prefer to see the state remain one large park.

Tourism, now Alaska's second largest industry, continues to increase. Ironically, the influx of visitors may be the chief force working to preserve native culture. Though living in a time of rapid transition, natives maintain their customs as a saleable commodity to tourists. How long this link to the past will continue is uncertain. But for the present, the dances, songs, games, carvings, and blanket tosses are authentic and very much in evidence.

Forward strides in transportation make it easy to reach Alaska and to get around. It's no longer a remote and isolated land; you don't have to be a rugged pioneer to visit. Accommodations can be as good as anywhere else in the U.S. (The seafood is better.) Everyone—from avid fisherman and backpacker to art collector and photographer—finds something of interest.

Among the state's greatest assets are the Alaskan residents. Friendly and outgoing, they tend to work as hard as they play. You'll find them courteous, helpful, and eager to talk about their land.

Something-for-everyone weather

Because of the state's great size, its ocean currents and mountain ranges, variety rules Alaska's weather. Contrary to popular belief, it is not a land of endless ice and snow. You'll discover grand rain forests and hillsides of wildflowers—even a desert in the Arctic.

Generally, the coastal and Aleutian areas have a wet maritime climate with suddenly surprising clear days. Mountains wear heavy snow capes. Warm summers and cold winters with low precipitation similar to the Dakotas mark the interior. In the Arctic there's low precipitation, windy cold winters, and cool summers.

When to visit Alaska

Alaska's diversity makes it possible to plan a vacation at any time of year, but the most popular tourist season is May to mid-October. Cruise ships navigate the Inside Passage waters only during this period; ferries operate all year but increase the number of sailings in summer.

Late spring and early fall are ideal travel months in most of the state. Normally favorable weather and especially colorful scenery mark spring and fall.

June, July, and August are peak tourist months. Lodges, restaurants, and sightseeing excursions swing into full operation. It's usually

Characteristic cross and onion dome distinguish Russian Orthodox churches throughout Alaska. St. Nicholas in Juneau is Southeast's oldest.

warm (hot in the interior) with short nights and long summer days.

For ski enthusiasts, dog sled fans, or snowshoe trekkers, though, an Alaskan winter vacation fills the bill. Alaska's largest ski area, Mt. Alyeska near Anchorage, takes you soaring 1¼ miles up on a double chair lift for a panoramic view of Turnagain Arm. Anchorage's Fur Rendezvous, a big winter celebration in February, features the World Championship Sled Dog Races.

Pick your living style

Whether you prefer to be pampered in elegant surroundings or to rough it in the backwoods, Alaska's lodgings can satisfy your needs. On cruises through Southeast Alaska your ship is your hotel—*and* your restaurant. Even ferries offer cabins and dining rooms on most sailings.

Hotel lodging. Accommodations in Alaska range from buildings that are ultra-new and modern to those still existing from pioneer days. Each year new hotels join other splendid ones in larger cities. But you'll still find old-time roadhouses left from dog mushing days. Most roadhouses have been modernized with electric lights and indoor plumbing.

Tour operators use much of the space in hotels during summer. If you're traveling independently, you'll have to reserve well in advance. Facilities engaged on tours, though usually comfortable, generally do not qualify as luxurious.

At Skagway, *visitor waves "goodbye" to departing ship. The marine highway connects Southeast communities.*

Wilderness lodges, tucked away in spots generally accessible only by air or by water, offer a sampling of Alaska's back country. Price usually includes comfortable rustic rooms and family style dining.

Camping. Alaska might well be considered one large campground. The 16 million acre Tongass National Forest in Southeast Alaska and the 2 million acre Chugach National Forest in south-central Alaska offer extensive recreational possibilities. (See page 25 for bargains in camping.)

Not surprisingly, Alaska's State Park System is America's largest. It boasts nearly 1.2 million acres of crystal clear waters for sailing among jewel-like islands, strategic waterfalls to serenade picnickers, and vantage points for photographing great moose and grizzly bear.

State parks, recreation areas, and highway waysides offer spaces on a first come, first served basis; no reservations are necessary at present. For current information on state campgrounds, write Alaska Division of Parks, 323 E. Fourth Ave., Anchorage, AK 99501. Further information on Alaska, including brochures and maps, can be obtained from the Alaska State Division of Tourism, Pouch E-WOA, Juneau, AK 98111.

Most public campgrounds contain picnic tables and shelters, outdoor toilets, well water, firepits, and firewood. Seasoned campers carry their own water and stoves for emergency uses.

Campgrounds usually designate trailer and motor home spaces, but you probably won't find hookups in public campgrounds.

Privately owned campgrounds operate in or near most towns and along the highways. Here you'll find individual hookups, as well as restrooms and showers.

In undeveloped sites, permits may be required to build campfires; check locally for information. Be sure your fire is out before you leave. Alaska's foliage and organic duff (ground cover) are very flammable, and fire fighting equipment may be several hundred miles away.

You can buy groceries in towns. Prices are higher than they are at home—from 15% to half again as much, depending on location. If your larder runs low while you're traveling, most lodges along the Alaska Highway also carry groceries and canned goods.

Mosquitos, deer flies, and a small biting fly (called "no-see-um" because you usually don't) are the camper's worst enemies during summer. If you camp in swampy areas or get into brush, protect yourself with head covering, gloves, and insect repellent. Tents with built-in insect netting are a wise choice for Alaska.

When you're in the back country, remember this is wildlife territory. Take precautions with food at your campsite; don't feed wild animals.

A touch of history

History credits no one person as the discoverer of Alaska. Before the arrival of Europeans, there had been Eskimos, Aleuts, and Indians living in some areas for 10,000 years or longer.

The proximity of the Seward Peninsula to Siberian coastline (some 56 miles) suggests that Alaska's first inhabitants came from Asia. Anthropologists believe that, no more than 25,000 years ago and no less than 12,000 years, Mongolian tribes migrated from Asia to America by way of the Bering Strait, an isthmus that at one time connected the two continents.

Alaska's rich historical background contains exotic overtones. In the early part of the 18th century, Russian Czar Peter the Great, who had a keen interest in geography, hired Danish Captain Vitus Bering to explore eastern waters. Bering "discovered" the Alaska mainland in 1741.

Captain James Cook visited Alaska's coastline in 1778, and other explorers investigated Alaska's waters, leaving British, French, and Spanish names on their charts.

By 1787, the Russians had a three-year-old settlement at Kodiak. Fur trade—especially of the highly prized sea otter—was vigorously exploited by the Russians in Alaska.

In 1806, Alexander Baranof, governor of Russian America, moved his headquarters from Kodiak to Sitka. This doughty little man ruled Alaska for 20 years. At the time of the California gold rush in 1849, Sitka was known as the "Paris of the Pacific" because it had all the pomp and gaiety of a European court.

Secretary of State William H. Seward negotiated the purchase of Alaska in 1867. Most Americans called the $7,200,000 purchase "Seward's Folly" and nicknamed the territory "Seward's Icebox."

Discovery of gold in the Cassiar country of British Columbia touched off a stampede in 1874–76. Most of the gold-seekers went in by way of Wrangell and the Stikine River. In 1880, gold was found near what is now Juneau. The great Treadwell and Alaska-Juneau mines were flourishing. Miners would work here for a grubstake to prospect in other areas, hoping to make

another big strike. It was the fabulous Klondike strike of 1896–98 that finally focused attention on the north.

Between 1900 and 1910 a series of gold discoveries from Nome to Fairbanks lured those in search of gold. Transportation was by sea and riverboat in summer and by dog team in winter.

Alaska was made a territory in 1912. Its first legislature met in 1913. Though Judge James Wickersham introduced the first statehood bill in the Congress in 1916, it was not until January, 1959, that statehood was finally achieved.

Meanwhile, in 1935, drought-stricken farmers from the Midwest settled the Matanuska Valley, introducing the state's first agriculture.

In 1942, during World War II, the Alaska Highway was built.

Some protection for the land claims of Alaskan natives was written into the Statehood Act. Recent developments and demands for land by public and private sources have caused the natives to give more thought to those ancestral hunting grounds.

In 1971, the Alaska Native Claims Settlement Act gave Eskimos, Aleuts, and Indians claim to 44 million acres, in addition to setting aside other lands for preservation.

What to wear, where

Casual, informal attire is the rule throughout Alaska. Emphasis is on sport clothes, though you'll probably want one dressy outfit if you plan to visit night spots in larger cities. Take a raincoat and a light wrap for cool evenings in summer. For visits to the warm interior, you'll want lightweight clothing. Comfortable walking shoes are a must.

Parkas are provided on Arctic excursions (boots in Barrow, if needed), but you may want to bring along your own gloves and warm caps.

Cruise passengers might add suits and ties or long dresses for special shipboard occasions. Deck shoes aid in walking slippery gangways.

Getting to Alaska

You can fly nonstop to Alaska from several cities within the other 49 states. Connecting flights from Seattle put all of Alaska's major towns and cities within three or four jet hours from anywhere. You might add Alaska as a stopover on an international flight to the Orient or Europe or as part of a triangle trip from the West Coast to Hawaii.

Sail the Inside Passage by ferry or cruise ship; drive or go by motor coach on the 1,523-mile Alaska Highway through Canada. Or combine highway, sea, and air routes for a personalized look at the state.

For specific information on services, facilities,

Fur hats, parkas, *coats, and toys win smiles of appreciation from shoppers in tourist stopovers.*

Lone boat *cruises along watery byways of Southeast's marine highway.*

and visitor attractions, write to the Alaska State Division of Tourism (Pouch E, Juneau, AK 99811) for a free booklet. To pick up latest folders and information on package itineraries and optional excursions, visit your travel agent.

By air

These U.S. carriers fly directly into Alaska: Alaska Airlines, Northwest Airlines, Western Airlines, and Wien Air Alaska.

Foreign carriers with stopovers in Anchorage on intercontinental flights include Air France, British Airways, Japan Air Lines, KLM, Korean Air Lines, Lufthansa, Sabena, and Scandinavian Airlines.

By sea

With possibilities in water travel ranging from small private boats to state ferries to luxurious cruise ships heading up the Inside Passage, your choice is wide.

The Alaska Marine Highway System provides scheduled water transportation (passengers and vehicles) from Prince Rupert, B.C., and Seattle to the Southeast Alaskan towns of Ketchikan, Wrangell, Petersburg, Sitka, Juneau, Haines, and Skagway, with connections to smaller communities.

A Canadian ferry carries travelers (including motorists) from Kelsey Bay, B.C. to Prince Rupert to connect with the Alaska ferry system.

(Continued on page 17)

Festivals & festivities

The listings below provide information on annual events and festivities of general interest to visitors. Dates change; it's advisable to check with the Chambers of Commerce of individual towns or the Alaska State Division of Tourism, Pouch E, Juneau, AK 99811.

JANUARY

Fairbanks—First sled dog race of the season.

Petersburg—World Championship King Salmon Derby.

FEBRUARY

Anchorage—Fur Rendezvous (Alaska's largest winter celebration) with World Championship Sled Dog Races, fur auction, Miners and Trappers Ball, Eskimo dances, wrestling, blanket-toss exhibitions, snowshoe baseball game, and parades.

Cordova—Iceworm Festival, celebrating iceworm's emergence from hibernation. Art show, skeet shoot, teen rodeo, queen's pageant, airboat races, ski events, crab-shaking contests, parades, dances.

Homer—Winter Carnival.

Whitehorse, Yukon—Winter Carnival "Sourdough Rendezvous."

MARCH

Dillingham—Beaver Roundup, with dog races, Eskimo dances and games, queen contest.

Fairbanks—North American Championship Sled Dog Races.

Juneau—Arts and Crafts show.

Nome—Golovin-Nome Snowmobile Classic (big prize snow machine race). Residents greet contestants finishing 1,000-mile Iditarod Sled Dog Race from Anchorage.

APRIL

Kenai—Kenai Peninsula Arts and Crafts show.

Nenana—Big Breakup (late April or early May) marks winter's end in Alaska's interior as well as the Nenana Ice Classic, one of the world's greatest public lotteries, begun in 1917 to relieve winter tedium. The total unpredictability of the lottery attracts statewide attention—and money.

Sitka—Fishermen's Festival. Blessing of the Fleet the first day of fishing season. Russian Easter celebration, cathedral services, bell playing.

MAY

Haines—Salmon Derby.

Kenai—Kenai Peninsula Trade Fair.

Petersburg—"Little Norway" Festival, celebrating first halibut landings, Armed Forces Day, and Norwegian Independence Day. Dancing, beach cookouts, smorgasbords, glacier tours, fishing.

JUNE

Anchorage—Festival of Music, including major concerts, recitals, lectures, visual arts, theater, and dance.

Fairbanks—Midnight Sun Baseball Festival (game played at midnight without artificial lights).

Gambell—Annual Whale Festival, featuring traditional whaling ceremonies.

Ketchikan—(June to mid-September) The Fish Pirate's Daughter melodrama.

Kodiak—Crab Festival with parades, world's championship seal-skinning contest, crowning of queen, crab race, and carnival.

Nome—Midnight Sun Festival includes raft race starting at midnight down Nome River, midnight baseball games, parade.

Palmer—Midsummer Festival features Scottish Games Championships, horse show, Grotto Lunkers competition with prizes for most original and gruesome paper maché creations.

Skagway—(June to mid-September) Mighty Moose Melodrama, Soapy Smith Show, and "Days of '98" with gambling and dancing.

JULY

Most Alaskan cities—Fourth of July celebrations, including parades, fireworks, evening dances.

Fairbanks—World Eskimo/Indian/Aleut Olympics, queen contest and competitive games focused on strength and endurance. Farthest North Flower Show. Golden Days, commemorating discovery of gold in 1902; old-timers' parade.

Haines—Haines Dalton Trail Days, old-time costumes, parade, midway, dances, contests.

Juneau—(late July to mid-August) Annual Golden North Salmon Derby.

Ketchikan—Logger's Rodeo.

Kotzebue—Fourth of July festival with dancing, high jumping, muktuk-eating contest, and queen contestants.

Seward—Mt. Marathon foot race.

Sitka—All Alaska Logging Championship.

AUGUST

Dawson City, Yukon—Discovery Day celebration, commemorating discovery of gold in the Klondike; includes Klondike Ball.

Fairbanks—Tanana Valley Fair with farm produce and animal exhibits, musical plays, pie-eating contests, foot races.

Haines—Southeast Alaska State Fair, horse show, world-famous Chilkat Dancers.

Homer—local agricultural products display.

Kodiak—"Cry of the Wild Ram," drama of early Russian America, and Baranof, presented by local residents in natural outdoor amphitheater.

Palmer—Alaska State Fair includes state's largest horse show, more than 5,000 exhibits of agriculture and homemaking.

Seward—Silver Salmon Derby, 24-hour-a-day fishing.

SEPTEMBER

Fairbanks—Annual Equinox Marathon (26-mile, 385-yard course over fields and hillsides near university campus).

Kodiak—Jaycee Rodeo.

OCTOBER

Sitka—Alaska Day Festival, commemorating transfer of Alaska from Russia to U.S. in 1867; traditional parade, Tlingit dances, Baranof's Ball.

DECEMBER

Christmas week in the Arctic features community celebrations with dancing; foot, dog sled, snowmobile races; Eskimo games with wrestling, finger-pulling, high kicking; almost continuous feasting.

An Alaskan vocabulary

As colorful as Alaska's history is the language of the state's residents. Some words are holdovers from frontier days; others are freshly coined to fit this unique land:

• *Alaskan horses:* folklore calls the summer pests, mosquitoes, "large enough to saddle."

• *black gold:* vast oil discoveries; North Slope oil flows through the state in an 800-mile-long pipeline.

• *breakup:* the spring event when ice-choked rivers start flowing; main celebration at Nenana.

• *bush pilots:* Alaska's "bird men"; they fly to all of the state's remote spots.

• *cabin fever:* the inability to get outside the house because of weather, ended only by summer's long daylight hours.

• *cache:* a miniature cabin built on stilts to keep food from animals; resembles a tall dog house.

• *calve:* the break-off of great pieces of glacial ice, producing large floes.

• *cheechako:* a newcomer to Alaska.

• *chill factor:* the wind's effect on temperature (30°F with wind speed of 30 mph gives actual temperature of −2°F).

• *Lower 48:* the continental United States.

• *midnight sun:* the longest day of the

year when the sun merely dips below the horizon to rise again.

• *Outside:* anywhere other than Alaska.

• *paydirt:* a mining term referring to placer gold.

• *permafrost:* permanently frozen ground, usually covered by a thin layer of tundra.

• *sourdough:* one who has weathered a winter; the term originated when prospectors took along their "starter."

• *termination dust:* the first snowfall, marking the beginning of winter.

...Continued from page 13

During summer, cruise ships sailing to Alaska from Vancouver, San Francisco, and Los Angeles visit most Southeastern cities on one or two-week cruises. Passengers may cruise round-trip or—to include a land and air exploration of other parts of the state—just one way.

Lines offering special cruises include Canadian Pacific Cruises, Holland America Cruises, March Shipping Lines, Paquet Ulysses Cruises, Princess Cruises, Royal Viking Lines, Sitmar Cruises, Westours, and World Explorer Cruises.

Seaplane *is your only transport to Golden Horn Lodge in remote western Alaska. Guide shows you trophy fishing spots.*

By bus

Westours operates a frequent motor coach tour service to Alaska from Seattle (summer only) in connection with other methods of transportation. Other tour operators offer charter motor coach tours from Seattle and Portland to Alaska. Usually part of a fixed-price itinerary, the package trip includes transportation, accommodations, sightseeing, baggage transfers, and some meals.

Coachways System, a division of Greyhound Lines of Canada, provides scheduled bus service between Canadian cities and Fairbanks.

Alaska - Yukon Motorcoaches (4th and Battery Bldg., Suite 555, Seattle, WA 98121) connects with the state ferries at Haines with scheduled service to Anchorage, Tok, and Fairbanks. Scheduled service is also available between Seattle and Alaska via Prince Rupert and the

Team 12 *hits the turn at North American Sled Dog Championship Races in Fairbanks (see "Festivals & festivities," page 14).*

Alaska Marine Highway System with calls at southeastern ports.

Driving the highways

Alaska's highways are referred to by name, not number. The primary road system consists of these highways: the Alaska, the Tok Cut-off, the Richardson, the Glenn, the Parks (Anchorage - Fairbanks), the Anchorage - Seward, the Sterling, the Carcross (connecting Skagway with Whitehorse), and the Haines. All of the roads are paved with the exception of the Canadian portions of the Haines Highway and much of the Alaska Highway.

The Haines Highway. You drive through scenic wilderness on this 159-mile highway that offers magnificent mountain views to delight the photographer. Much of the route follows the old Dalton Trail to the Klondike, climbing steeply from coastal timber country to Chilkoot Pass and high meadows above timberline.

From Haines, Alaska (where you disembark from an Inside Passage ferry), it is 42 miles to the Canadian border (see Canadian customs requirements, this page). Near Haines is a 2-mile detour taking you through the old Chilkat Indian village of Klukwan. Scattered along the road are a few places to stay. At Mosquito Lake there's a public campground, reached by a 2½-mile side road that leaves the highway 27 miles from Haines.

In autumn, winter, or early spring, be sure to find out about current highway conditions before leaving Haines. In the Yukon this highway becomes Yukon Highway 4. At Haines Junction turn left to join the Alaska Highway or right to visit Whitehorse, capital of Yukon Territory.

The Alaska Highway. Driving the Alaska Highway can be a wonderful adventure if you plan carefully and follow a few basic rules. It's not a hazardous journey, but it is a long one—1,523 miles from Mile 0 at Dawson Creek, B.C., to Fairbanks, Alaska. Your route takes you through mountains, over mighty rivers, through long stretches of virgin wilderness, past fishing streams and trading posts. The drive can be made in 5 to 7 days each way. If you allow three or four weeks for the round trip, though, you'll have more time to enjoy the scenery.

All but 300 miles of the road lies in Canada, where it was punched through as a military link during World War II. Although each year the road is additionally blacktopped and improved, primarily it is a good gravel road to the Alaska border. From the border to Fairbanks, the road is paved. Service stations and auto repair facilities are located at convenient intervals—never more than 25 to 50 miles apart.

The Alaska Highway remains open all year except for times when weather forces temporary closing. June through August attracts most travelers. Insects and dust are summer problems; use insect repellent and protect clothing from dust with zippered plastic bags. Tightly closed canisters or plastic bags keep dust out of food, cameras, and other articles. (Some motorists seal the car trunk with tape to protect luggage from dust.)

Motorists should get a cover for the underside of the gas tank to protect it from flying gravel. Plastic guards will protect headlights from rock breakage; bug screens will reduce damage from flying stones and protect automobile finish.

Mid-July to mid-September is probably the most pleasant time to drive the highway: less traffic, cooler days, no insects, and hillsides ablaze with golden splashes of aspen and birch. You may run into seasonal rains and some snow in higher passes. Late in the season, carry tire chains, a tow rope, and a shovel.

Winter travel is not recommended for a pleasure trip, and spring thaw (March through April) should be avoided. Washouts, detours, and road construction are common obstacles.

For mile-by-mile information on facilities and attractions along the Alaska Highway, look at a copy of *The Milepost*, published by Alaska Northwest Publishing Company.

Canadian customs. You'll go through customs when you cross the border. No passports are required by permanent U.S. citizens, but citizenship must be established by other documents, such as a birth certificate or a voter's registration. Naturalized citizens should carry naturalization papers; resident aliens must have an Alien Registration Receipt Card. Vehicle permits, issued free at the border, are necessary for Canadian travel. Be sure to carry your motor vehicle registration form. Check with your insurance company on coverage in Canada.

These are the duty free articles you may take into Canada: personal belongings (including radios, cameras, and reasonable food supplies); sporting goods (firearms subject to special restrictions); up to 50 cigars, 200 cigarettes, 2 pounds of tobacco, and 40 ounces of alcoholic beverages per adult. Returning U.S. residents may bring one quart of liquor and 100 cigars per adult. There's no limit on cigarettes.

Package itineraries

Package vacations are probably the best way to see Alaska with the least amount of effort. In the variety they offer, these tours are unique. Most excursions include various combinations of cruise ship/ferry, airline, motor coach, and rail transportation. Some itineraries are escorted; others simply offer transportation and accommodations for visitors who wish to travel more independently.

Package vacations ranging from a week to a month or longer vary in itineraries and prices according to tour operators and options. For colorful brochures and specific information, see your travel agent or write to the following major tour operators:
• Maupintour, Box 807, Lawrence, KS 66044
• Alaska Tour & Marketing Services, Suite 312, Park Place Bldg., Seattle, WA 98101
• Alaska Travel Bureau, 1030 Washington Bldg., Seattle, WA 98101
• Green Carpet Tours and Kneisel Travel, 345 N.E. Eighth Ave., Portland, OR 97232
• Greyhound World Tours, 8th & Stewart Sts., Seattle, WA 98101
• Johansen Royal Tours, 1410 Vance Bldg., Seattle, WA 98101
• Princess Tours, 727 Washington Bldg., Seattle, WA 98101
• Travalaska Tours, Suite 470, Fourth & Vine Bldg., Seattle, WA 98121
• Westours, 300 Elliot Ave. W., Seattle, WA 98119.
• World Explorer Cruises, Taj Mahal Bldg., Box 2428, Laguna Hills, CA 92653

Moving around in Alaska

From earlier reliance on boat and dog team travel, the transportation picture within Alaska has changed rapidly during the past 30 years, thanks to the airplane and automobile. Construction of the Alaska Highway from Dawson Creek, B.C., to Fairbanks during 1942-43 gave Alaska a land link with the continental road system and stimulated further road building. Bus lines and railroad routes lace the state. The state ferry system in southeastern Alaska provides a "marine highway" to ports in that part of the state. Regular jet airlines serve main towns and cities, and competent bush pilots—Alaska's bird men—reach the most remote villages. You can charter a plane in almost any town to fly almost anywhere.

Airlines maintain regular service to cities, towns, and villages throughout Alaska. The three largest are Alaska Airlines, Wien Air Alaska, and Reeve Aleutian Airways.

Buses operating within the state include Alaska Hyway Tours (between Skagway and Anchorage, and between Anchorage and Valdez), Alaska-Yukon Motorcoaches (between Haines and Anchorage, and between Anchorage and Fairbanks via Mt. McKinley National Park), Transportation Services (routes between Anchorage and Seward, Homer, Valdez, and intermediate points), and Westours Motor Coaches (Anchorage to Fairbanks, Anchorage to Valdez, Anchorage and Fairbanks to Mt. McKinley National Park, and Fairbanks or Valdez to Whitehorse, B.C.).

Rail travel plays an important part in touring the state. Railroading here has a special luster in these times when passenger travel by rail in other parts of the U.S. is declining.

The Alaska Railroad serves Anchorage, Mt. McKinley National Park, Fairbanks, and points along the way. From Anchorage it runs south to Portage and Whittier.

The narrow-gauge White Pass & Yukon Railway operates the year around between Skagway and Whitehorse, Y.T. During summer, special one-day, round-trip excursions depart Skagway to follow the Klondike miners' trail.

Both rail routes cross impressive mountain ranges. Advance reservations are not required; tickets must be purchased at the depot prior to departure. You can ship cars on both lines.

Alaska marine ferries connect ports on Cook Inlet (Homer, Kodiak, and Seldovia) and Prince William Sound (Cordova, Valdez, and summertime service to Whittier) on the *M/V Tustumena* and *M/V Bartlett*. This Southcentral System does not connect with Southeast Alaska ferries.

Car, camper, and motor home rental is possible at various locations throughout the state. It may be possible for you to rent in one city and "drop off" in another. Rental vehicles are limited; advance reservations are recommended during peak summer months. Reservations may be made through travel agents or local representatives of national firms: Avis, Budget, Hertz, and National. Anchorage is headquarters for Airways Rent a Car, Alpha/One Car Rental System, and Captain Cook Car Rentals. Sport & Travel Equipment Co. in Anchorage rents only campers and motor homes.

Alaska's stunning outdoors

Alaska is a sportsman's paradise. For the hunter there are the famous Alaska brown bears, grizzly and black bears, moose, goats, mountain sheep, and other trophy animals. Tempting lakes, streams, and rivers await the fisherman. Uncrowded ski slopes invite skiers. And for the hiker and nature lover, a vast world of imposing scenery beckons.

Wildlife watching

If nightlife is not Alaska's trump card, wildlife certainly is. An alert visitor can often sight

moose, bear, mountain sheep, and caribou from the road. You may also see bright-eyed fox, an occasional coyote or wolf, the tiny pika, marmot, Dall sheep (on coastal peaks), beaver, otter, marten, mink, and hare.

The Arctic has walrus, seals, polar bears, foxes, caribou, mountain sheep, whales, and many smaller animals, such as the lemming.

Mt. McKinley National Park is Alaska's most substantial game refuge. For a description of the wildlife there, see page 58; also see special feature on page 100.

Most of Alaska's summer bird life consists of migratory waterfowl who come north to nest, but watchers can find eagles and many kinds of hawks, jays, owls, spruce hens, and grouse, in addition to the ptarmigan—the state bird—and many common small birds.

The Pribilof Islands offer some of the world's greatest birdwatching. Here even an amateur ornithologist becomes an avid tracker. Here, too, you'll see the world's largest fur seal herd.

Fishing and hunting

Alaska's fishing and hunting lodges and resorts are scattered throughout the state, and bush pilots fly sportsmen into virgin wilderness areas.

The Alaska Department of Fish & Game (Information Section, Subport Bldg., Juneau, AK 99811) provides free pamphlets on hunting and sportfishing seasons, bag and creel limits, licenses and tag fees, tips on best fishing areas, and a list of guides (required for big game hunting).

Fishermen find salmon in all coastal waters and most streams. In southeastern Alaska, the ocean waters host all five Alaskan species of salmon: chum, king, pink, red, and silver. High on the list is the king salmon, also called tyee or chinook. Starting in April, fish show in increasing numbers. Kings range from 10 to 40 pounds and larger; silver are smaller but noted for their spectacular acrobatics when hooked. Bottom fish—including red snapper, ling cod, halibut, and rockfish—also lure anglers.

Freshwater streams, lakes, and saltwater estuaries offer cutthroat and rainbow, as well as Dolly Varden, Arctic char, grayling, and pike.

Central and southwestern Alaska is generally regarded as the best freshwater sportfishing region in the state. Dedicated fly fishermen will want to sample the streams of Iliamna Lake on the Alaska Peninsula and in Katmai National Monument. Highway travelers' best fishing spots are the freshwater lakes and streams on the Kenai Peninsula and the marine waters of Cook Inlet and Prince William Sound.

In the far north, the exotic sheefish (a cross between tarpon and whitefish) are abundant. Migrating in large numbers up major river systems, they provide challenging sport for anglers. Sheefish may be taken from May through September, though July is the peak fishing time. You'll probably need an air charter to reach a wilderness lodge.

Hiking and canoeing

A few minutes' hike from any road or town puts you into Alaska's wilderness. Unless you are an experienced woodsman, it is not advisable to go hiking alone. Particularly popular hikes are in areas such as Mt. McKinley National Park, Chugach State Park, and the Kenai Peninsula.

Those who seek areas off the beaten path can test their skills in Katmai or Glacier Bay national monuments. For vacations involving unconventional travel into remote areas, visitors should select knowledgeable guides.

If you want to travel by water, guides will take you on canoe, kayak, or raft trips on many of Alaska's thousands of rivers and lakes.

Skiing

Ski areas in Alaska center around the cities of Anchorage and Fairbanks. The largest and most developed ski spot is Mt. Alyeska, 38 miles south of Anchorage. Airlines offer ski packages.

Elsewhere in the state, skiing takes place at Harriet Hunt Ski Area near Ketchikan; the new Eaglecrest resort at Juneau; and Eyak Mountain, near Cordova.

Ply a canoe *through the waterways of Kenai National Moose Range for a rare wilderness experience.*

Southeast: the Panhandle

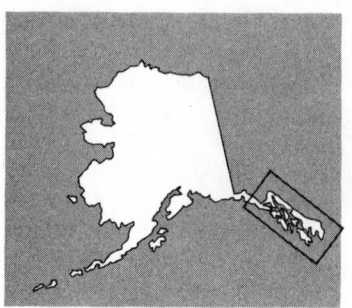

Alaska's Panhandle, a narrow lacework of islands and peninsulas, stretches 400 miles down the seacoast at the base of the towering Coastal Range. On the other side lies Canada.

Huge, ice-age glaciers scraped and sculptured this land, carving deep canyons that lead to the sea. Remnants of these ice rivers cling to mountain tops and poke blue-white fingers down their sides.

Densely forested slopes drop sharply toward the shore. A few settlements, dwarfed by their vertical backdrops, cling to narrow strips of flat land two or three blocks wide and stretch out for miles. Juneau, dubbed "The Longest City in the World," strings along the shore for 40 miles; Ketchikan extends for 20 miles. Skagway, northernmost port town, appears wedged among towering peaks.

Considered by many Alaska's most scenically beautiful region, the Southeast is easy to visit—less than two hours by jet or three days by ferry or cruise ship from the Pacific Northwest.

Throughout Southeast Alaska you'll find remnants of three cultures: totems from Alaska's Indian heritage, Russian Orthodox churches from the days when the Czar ruled these lands, and frontier villages from the era when the cry of "gold" was heard to the north.

Accommodations range from modern city hotels to rustic cabins on secluded bays. In some hotels you might feel you are paying a bit steeply for a room that wouldn't measure up to deluxe standards at home. But, on the other side of the scale, you can also reserve a cottage for the modest price of $5 a night (see page 25).

The weather? Warmed by ocean currents and shielded from the ocean by offshore islands, the Southeast rarely suffers temperature extremes. Winter temperatures seldom drop below 10° F., and summer temperatures average between 60-70°. In winter, snow falls mainly in higher elevations.

You can expect rain any month of the year, usually daily from fall to spring.

Ketchikan boasts of their annual average of 13 feet; Juneau records 90 inches a year. Skagway, though, receives a moderate 27 inches of rainfall. Like many Hawaiians, Alaskans have learned to live with the rain. Fishermen still fish; lumber mills continue producing pulp; and children splash in puddles outdoors. On the many days of glorious sunshine you reap the benefits—exaggerated clarity of color and clear air.

A watery highway

You can't travel through Southeast Alaska by road. Only ships and planes connect Southeast communities.

Alaska Airlines flies between Anchorage and Seattle with stops at Juneau, Sitka, Petersburg, Wrangell and Ketchikan. Wien Air Alaska flies from Fairbanks or Whitehorse (in the Yukon) to Juneau and from Anchorage to Seattle via Juneau and Ketchikan. Western Airlines stops at Juneau en route to Anchorage from Seattle.

But the water route is the classic one. Ever since the Tlingit Indians hollowed out their first canoes centuries ago, the Inside Passage has been Southeast Alaska's chief highway. For over 200 years it was the main artery of commerce and exploration for both Russian traders and American explorers.

Now, for many adventurous visitors, the marine highway serves as an introduction to the state. Both sleek cruise ships and modern ferries ply the 1,000-mile sheltered waterway maze.

Whether you decide to travel by cruise liner or ferry, Southeast Alaska is best seen from the deck

Harbor view *shows how Juneau strings along base of towering Mt. Juneau and Mt. Roberts.*

Southeast Alaska

Skagway—Reminder of Gold Rush days

"Days of '98" variety show
Gold Rush cemetery
Klondike National Park
Mighty Moose Melodrama
Soapy Smith show
White Pass & Yukon Railway

Haines/Port Chilkoot—scenic area with native dancers and crafts

Alaska Indian Arts Center
Chilkat Dancers
Totem Village

Glacier Bay National Monument—relics of an ice age

Air tours of ice fields
Cruises on sightseeing boat
Fishing from Bartlett Cove

Juneau—Alaska's capital city

Alaska State Museum
House of Wickersham
Mendenhall Glacier
Red Dog Saloon

Sitka—Russian-American heritage

New Archangel Dancers in Centennial Building
St. Michael's Cathedral
Sheldon Jackson Museum
Sitka National Historic Park

Petersburg—Alaska's "Little Norway"

Le Conte Glacier air and boat trips
Norwegian Festival in May
Petersburg Museum

Wrangell—waterfront canneries, lumber mills, and boat harbors

Chief Shake's Island
Wrangell Museum

Ketchikan—salmon fishing center

Dolly's House on Creek Street
Saxman Park
Tongass Historical Society Museum
Totem Bight State Park
Totem Heritage Center

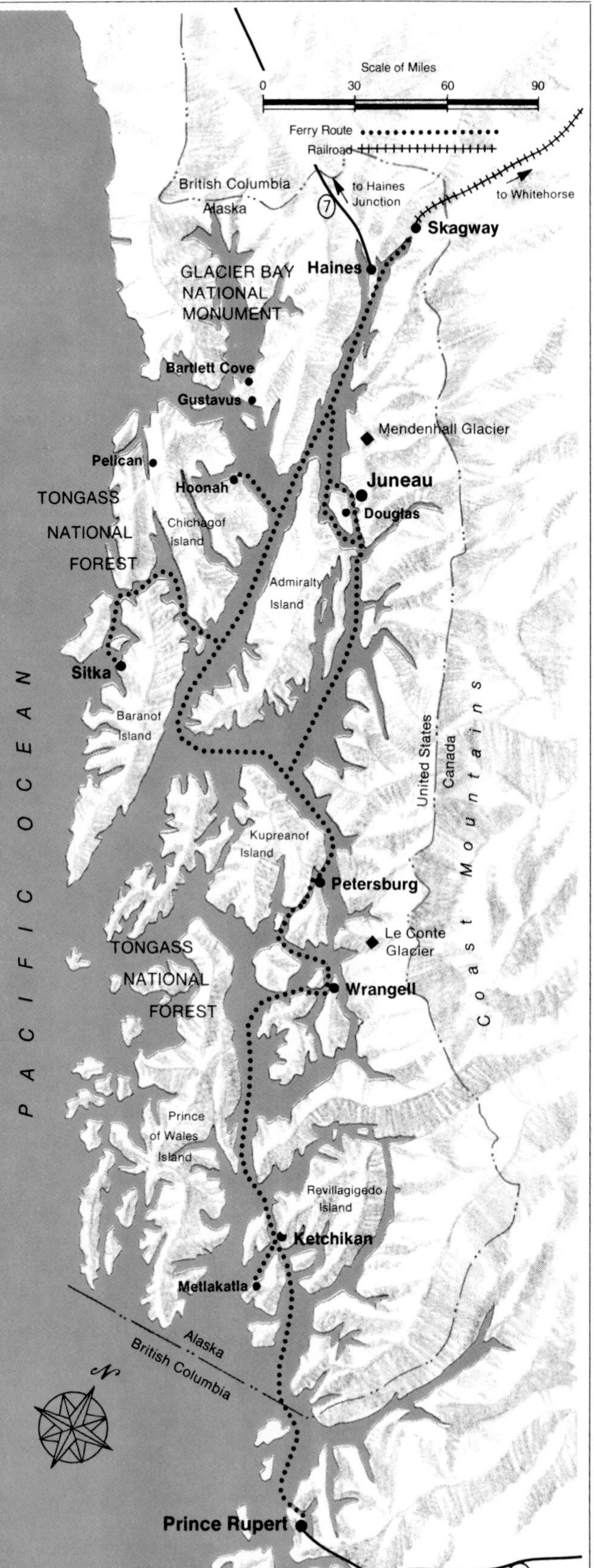

Scale of Miles
0   30   60   90

Ferry Route ••••••••••
Railroad ++++++++++

British Columbia
Alaska

to Haines
Junction

to Whitehorse

Skagway

Haines

GLACIER BAY
NATIONAL
MONUMENT

Bartlett Cove
Gustavus

Mendenhall Glacier

Pelican

TONGASS

Hoonah

Juneau

NATIONAL

Chichagof
Island

Douglas

FOREST

Admiralty
Island

Sitka

Baranof
Island

United States
Canada

Coast Mountains

Kupreanof
Island

Petersburg

Le Conte
Glacier

TONGASS

NATIONAL

Wrangell

FOREST

Prince
of Wales
Island

Revillagigedo
Island

Ketchikan

Metlakatla

Alaska
British Columbia

N

Prince Rupert

PACIFIC OCEAN

Wilderness bargain lodging

If you're a traveler who wants to visit some of Alaska's more remote regions, you will find handy and inexpensive accommodations in Tongass and Chugach national forests. If you don't mind roughing it a bit, for only $5 a day you can rent a primitive cabin in the wilderness of either forest.

More than 130 cabins are available in Tongass National Forest and about 30 in Chugach National Forest. In most cases you reach Tongass cabins by charter boat or float plane from the nearest town. Charters will be the most expensive portion of your vacation.

Cabins, ranging from rustic log structures to A-frames, will usually accommodate four persons comfortably. Some can handle up to 12 people.

All are equipped with bunks and pit toilets. Most have plank floors; none has electricity. Visitors must provide camping gear, bedding, food, and utensils (including a cookstove and an axe for chopping firewood).

Most of the cabins are on remote lakes or isolated bays and inlets. In many cases, you'll have the lake or stretch of coastline to yourself. A skiff is included as part of the equipment for all cabins situated on the water. Skiffs can accept outboard motors up to 7½ hp.

You must bring your own Coast Guard-approved flotation gear and outboard motors if you plan to boat or fish. You'll also need an Alaska fishing license.

Make reservations about six months in advance, indicating alternate cabin choices in case your first choice is not available.

Both forests will send on request a detailed map marking cabin locations and a reservation application. Deposits equaling the full rental price are required. Use permits for Tongass sites are limited to 7 days between April 1 and October 31 and to 10 days during the rest of the year. Chugach "hike-in" cabins have a 3-day limit between May 15 and August 31, and a 7-day limit the rest of the year.

For cabin information, write the Forest Supervisor at the following addresses: Tongass National Forest, Box 1628, Juneau, AK 99802; Chugach National Forest, Pouch 6606, Anchorage, AK 99504.

of a ship. An ever-changing panorama of cloud-shrouded islands, jagged mountains, spectacular fiords, and crevassed glaciers passes alongside.

Wildlife is abundant. Occasionally small pods of killer whales surface, porpoises ride the pressure wave off the bow, and a variety of birds—including the rare bald eagle—soar gracefully overhead. Sharing the waters are commercial fishermen trolling for salmon, laying deep halibut lines, and hauling in pots of Dungeness crab.

Choose your cruise

Cruise ships offer more than 100 separate sailings during the season from May to October. Leaving Vancouver, B.C., and, more infrequently from Los Angeles and San Francisco, ships stop in major Southeast communities. Some cruise lines combine the Inside Passage sailing with cruising in Glacier Bay National Monument.

Passengers may cruise round-trip or one-way, adding on an excursion by land or air to other parts of Alaska. The shortest round-trip cruise to Alaska is 7 days and includes stops at three or four ports. Some lines offer greatly reduced fares on early and late season sailings.

Be sure the cruise you pick includes the towns you want to visit. Some tours visit Prince Rupert and Alert Bay, B.C., in addition to Skagway and Juneau. Others may stop in Ketchikan and Haines, or include Victoria, B.C., in their cruise. Still others may turn around at Juneau, sending a sight-seeing excursion boat to Skagway for those pas-

Hearty hug *and kiss greets 22-pound king salmon after valiant 17-minute struggle at Glacier Bay.*

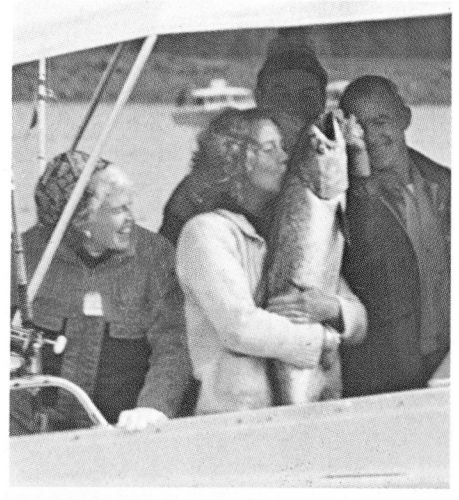

Business *along Ketchikan's once-lively Creek Street has dropped off; now only salmon come upstream.*

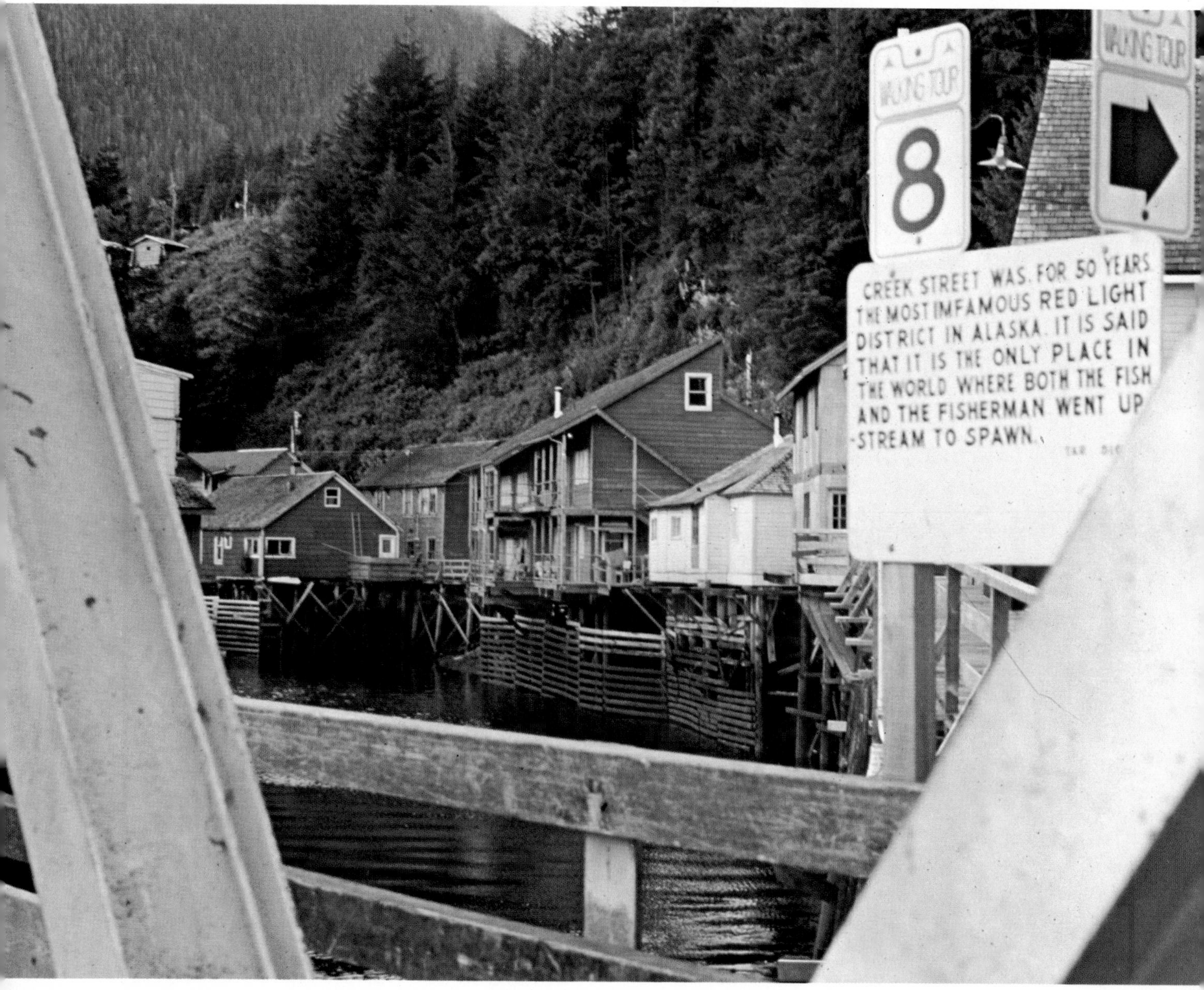
WALKING TOUR
8
CREEK STREET WAS. FOR 50 YEARS
THE MOST IMFAMOUS RED LIGHT
DISTRICT IN ALASKA. IT IS SAID
THAT IT IS THE ONLY PLACE IN
THE WORLD WHERE BOTH THE FISH
AND THE FISHERMAN WENT UP
-STREAM TO SPAWN.

sengers taking the White Pass & Yukon Railway or a motorcoach into the Interior. Some cruises continue on to Anchorage.

Remember that a ship is not only a form of transportation; it is a personal destination of its own. So choose one that suits you. For brochures and schedules, check with your travel agent or write to tour operators listed on page 20.

Alaska's ferry system

A fleet of six modern ferries efficiently shuttles passengers and vehicles from Seattle and Prince Rupert, B.C., to Southeast ports of Haines, Juneau, Ketchikan, Petersburg, Skagway, Sitka, and Wrangell. Connections can be made to smaller communities.

The largest liner, the *M/V Columbia*, has a passenger capacity of 1,000 people; the smallest, the *M/V Chilkat*, carries 75. Larger ferries provide limited cabins, restaurants, and lounges; all have observation decks and some type of food and beverage service.

Ferries operate throughout the year. Reduced rates are available off-season from October to May. You can arrange to stop at any port, picking up a later ferry to continue your trip; but you'll need to plan ahead and make your reservations accordingly. There is no extra charge for stopover privileges.

If you take your car, you can continue north from Haines by highway to Haines Junction on the Alaska Highway (where you either drive north to Fairbanks or start your return trip south). If you leave the ferry at Skagway, you can ship your car by rail on the White Pass & Yukon to Whitehorse on the Alaska Highway.

Reservations are required for staterooms and vehicles. For information on ferry schedules, write to the Department of Transportation and Public Facilities, Division of Marine Highway Systems, Pouch R, Juneau, AK 99811.

Panhandle waterfront ports

Southern Panhandle cities are among the oldest in the state. Some date from Indian days; some were Russian communities; others were born because of fishing, logging, or the search for gold. Artless in layout, the ports have streets that wander about like drunken miners. Buildings are wedged in where there is space. These cities show surprisingly little sign of change.

Ketchikan—gateway for fishermen

Busy, bustling Ketchikan terms itself the "Gateway to Alaska." It is, indeed, often a visitor's first stop.

Surrounded by water (it's on Revillagigedo Island), the town appears to cling to the edge of a dark green velvet mantle flowing from the shoulders of 3,000-foot Deer Mountain just before it trails into the Tongass Narrows. Much of the city's business district hangs suspended above water on pilings driven into the bottom of the Narrows; many homes are perched on cliffs reached by wooden staircases or narrow, winding streets.

Its good fishing waters have earned Ketchikan another title—"Salmon Capital of the World." Many sport fishermen arrive to try their luck in these prime waters.

Another claim that you would think Ketchikan residents would try to softpedal is that it has the highest rainfall per year of anywhere in Alaska. Instead, the citizens stage a lottery to guess annual precipitation and display a logo showing the "Ketchikan Rainbird" with umbrella held high.

Ketchikan and Juneau are fighting it out for the title of Alaska's third largest city. Depending on where you are, you'll hear one or the other claim being supported.

White steam plumes rising from a pulp mill, blue smoke curling up from a lumber mill, and a forest of fishing boat masts in the harbor reveal the town's economy.

Ships dock in the city's watery "front yard." Amphibious aircraft, like huge geese, land and take off from the waterfront, providing a major transportation link with outlying villages and fishing camps. If you arrive by airline across the Narrows, you can take a bus or taxi into town, including a short crossing on the local shuttle ferry.

Lodging and meals are available on a fairly limited basis. You'll find a handful of motels and hotels (usually with dining room and cocktail lounge) downtown. Fishermen usually head out to Clover Pass Resort, about 15 miles north from town, where they'll find a lodge, cabins, restaurant, and lounge—along with all facilities for fishing.

Campers and picnickers have a choice of several Forest Service sites not far by road from downtown. Groceries in Ketchikan are probably priced lower than anywhere else in Alaska.

Highlights of the area are covered by sightseeing bus or walking tour. You can get an excellent pamphlet that covers major points of interest in an hour's walk from the Visitors Bureau at the dock or from the Chamber of Commerce office on Mission near Main.

In this land of totems, you'll find several good displays. Totem Bight State Park, 11 miles north of Ketchikan, raises a number of poles, as well as a reproduction of a tribal house. Saxman Park, a few miles south of the city, displays a few poles—all well-done replicas.

For a quick background on the whys and wherefores of these handsomely carved "stories in wood," visit Ketchikan's handsome Cultural Heritage Center. Here, visitors can view some of the few remaining truly original totem poles brought in from abandoned Tlingit and Haida villages for protection from vandalism and from the elements.

The Centennial Museum Library Building on Dock Street, built to commemorate the 100-year anniversary of the purchase of Alaska from Russia, displays some interesting Tlingit, Haida, and Tsimshian arts and crafts; Russian relics; and photographs of old-time Ketchikan. The Ketchikan Indian Museum, also on Dock Street, houses a large collection of Indian artifacts.

Don't miss Creek Street, once the town's notorious red light district. Running along Ketchikan Creek, it's a collection of wooden houses and shops joined by boardwalks resting on pilings. Dolly's House, home of one of the last of the madams, has been restored to look as it did before the lady retired.

At the Frontier Saloon downtown watch the melodrama "The Fish Pirate's Daughter."

Shopping in Ketchikan is much like it is anywhere in Southeast Alaska. Best buys might be an Indian woven cedar basket, an original silk screen item from Northland Studio, gold nugget jewelry, or Eskimo and Indian carvings. If you're looking for a replica of a totem pole, you'll find one in almost every store.

Side trips might include chartering a boat for saltwater fishing or a plane to take you to upland lakes and trout streams. Regularly scheduled air service takes you to Bell Island Hot Springs Resort, Waterfall Cannery resort, or Yes Bay Lodge for fishing and relaxing. Or try a fishing trip by air to Humpback Lake Chalet or Prince of Wales Island. Charter flights to wilderness lakes or charter fishing boats can be arranged out of Ketchikan.

Wrangell—a friendly town

Still lightly touched by tourist trade, Wrangell lies 80 miles northwest of Ketchikan. It rests between the green forest and blue water, hugging the rim of a jewel-like harbor not far from the mouth of the Stikine River. Lumber mills, shrimp and salmon canneries, cold storage plants, and boat shops dominate the waterfront. Shops, bars, and stores line the one main street. Houses dot the hillside without much regard for planned streets.

The Stikine ("great river") played an important part in the history of Alaska's third oldest settlement. Today, big oil tanks stand on the site of an old Russian fort and trading post established in 1834. The fort, later occupied by England's Hudson Bay Company, became the U.S. Army's Fort Wrangell in 1868. Those were the days of fur trade, much of it stemming from the upper river.

Two gold rushes touched this settlement—first in 1874-76 with the discovery in the Cassiar, then again in 1897-1900 when miners stampeded through Wrangell, utilizing the Stikine River to reach the Klondike.

Alaska's first Protestant (Presbyterian) church was established here in 1879, the same year that famed naturalist John Muir visited the area.

Accommodations include a modern motel and an inn with restaurant and cocktail lounge. Hospitality is still on a very personal basis; residents extend a warm welcome to visitors. A number of small restaurants feature fresh seafood.

Highlights of this compact little town are conveniently close together, making walking easy. Near the harbor is the site of Bear Tribal House on Chief Shake's Island. Inside this reconstructed Indian ceremonial house fronted by totems, you'll gaze at tools, carvings, and other artifacts. Sightseeing tours stop here, as well as at one of Alaska's largest lumber mills, a salmon processing plant, and other points of interest.

Flightseeing tours take you over the Stikine Ice Fields, float planes follow the river, and charter air service transports you to LeConte Glacier, the southernmost of Alaska's tidewater glaciers.

Friendly Wrangell residents usually greet ships. Indian women spread their wares—beadwork, moccasins, shell jewelry, and other items—on the dock, and children sell wildflowers and native garnets. Gift shops along Front Street feature Alaskan designs and locally made jewelry, ceramics, and art work.

Wrangell has a salmon derby each summer involving special derby days and weekly prizes.

Petersburg—a Scandinavian flavor

Located on Mitkof Island, some 40 miles (10 minutes jet flight) northwest of Wrangell, Petersburg appears to be a bit of old Scandinavia, with its colorful fishing fleet at anchor or moving in and out with the tides. Fishing is the backbone of the town's economy. Salmon and shrimp canneries, cold storage plants, and docks form the waterfront on 21-mile Wrangell Narrows, a picturesque waterway.

Since its founding in 1891 by Norwegian immigrant Peter Buschmann, Petersburg has retained an appearance and friendliness that earned it the designation "Little Norway." Its brightly painted houses and colorful gardens set it apart from other Southeast Alaska communities. Many yachts make it a stopping place.

Accommodations vary from a small hotel and motels to an old cannery remodeled into an attractive inn. A number of restaurants feature fresh-from-the-sea and Scandinavian dishes.

There are facilities for large trailers at Island Trailer Court and for campers, tents, or small trailers at Fort Magill Camper Park, two blocks from the ferry terminal. Ohmer Creek Forest Service campground is 21 miles southeast of town on the Mitkof Highway.

Highlights of your visit to Petersburg might include a charter boat or air trip to fishing waters and hunting grounds or a day cruise to active LeConte Glacier, which spits icebergs into a small bay. During spawning season, you can watch salmon climb Falls Creek fish ladder. Visitors are welcome to tour Petersburg Fisheries cannery at 2 P.M. Monday through Friday.

In few Alaskan communities is a walking tour quite as rewarding. Along the waterfront you can view salmon, halibut, shrimp, crab, and scallops being processed. The Petersburg Museum houses the world-record 126-pound king salmon. In addition, the museum contains interesting artifacts of early Alaska fisheries and a section devoted to Indian fishing techniques. You'll also find the city's information center in the museum.

A special event takes place on May 17 when Petersburg holds a Norwegian Festival to celebrate Norway's Independence Day. It's a colorful festival with old-country costumes, dances, singing, fish fries, and a band concert.

Sitka: last Russian outpost

One of Southeast Alaska's most scenic and historic cities, Sitka puts on an attractive appearance for every visitor. It's easily reached by ferry, cruise ship, or scheduled air service. Beautifully situated against its backdrop of mountains, Sitka looks out over the sea to Mt. Edgecumbe, an extinct volcano that might be a twin to Japan's Mt. Fujiyama. Many little islands cluster in the harbor. A 3-hour boat cruise gives you a close look.

Sheltered dry dock *in Ketchikan keeps commercial fishing boat above the tide and protects workers from frequent blustery weather.*

History marks Sitka, probably Alaska's most historically interesting town. Founded in 1799 by Alexander Baranof and Russian settlers and trappers, Sitka was the capital of a Russian fur-trading empire that once reached as far south as Fort Ross in northern California. Today, vestiges of this occupation are still evident.

In the Tlingit Indian language "Sitka" means "in this place," and this place became Fort Archangel Michael for 68 years.

The town was transferred from Russia to the United States on October 18, 1867, in tearful ceremonies held on Keekor Hill—a huge boxlike rock (behind the post office) where Baranof's castle once stood. The site commands an impressive view of the town, the bay, and the old parade ground. One caution: Expect to climb a lot of stairs to reach the top of Keekor Hill.

Designs on downtown storefronts, the replica of a Russian fort's blockhouse, and the original Russian cemetery add to the foreign feeling.

Commercial fishing and a Japanese pulp mill operation once provided the basis of local economy, but Sitka is rapidly becoming a Navy town. The U.S. government operates a hospital and boarding school for Alaska natives, and the Presbyterian Church maintains Sheldon Jackson Junior College.

Hotel accommodations are gradually being expanded. Newest hotels are the Sheffield House on the waterfront and the Shee Atika Lodge downtown. Overnight visitors should have confirmed reservations. Rental cars are available. If you're planning an extensive stay, a car will come in handy.

In forests near town you'll find U.S. Forest Service campgrounds. Several downtown restaurants offer good dining. Again, seafood is a specialty; small Sitka abalone is a local delicacy.

Highlights of Sitka can be reached on foot or by sightseeing tour. The main attraction of any visit takes place on the stage of the convention center (Centennial Building), where visitors are welcomed by the New Archangel Dancers. These performances of Russian ethnic folk dances (shown when ships are in port) recall Sitka's glittering past.

Some of Sitka's earlier brilliance may also be viewed in the reconstructed St. Michael Russian Orthodox Cathedral. Built between 1844 and 1848 and often described as the finest example of Russian architecture in the United States, the cathedral was carefully rebuilt through community effort after a fire in 1966. Most of the vestments, marriage crowns, and beautifully detailed icons (valued at $1.5 million) were saved and are now on display.

Few Alaskan towns have such a variety of attractive museums. At the Centennial Building you'll find a historical exhibit including furniture from Baranof's original castle, old mining tools, and the like. By following a landscaped esplanade from the convention center to Sheldon Jackson Museum, you'll view a rich collection of Eskimo and Indian masks, as well as ancient artifacts and relics of early days. Only space prevents a more elaborate display.

At the sparkling new Visitors Center at Sitka National Historical Park, not far from the main part of town, people, pamphlets, and excellent exhibits give you background for getting the most out of your visit.

This 54-acre park, proclaimed a national monument in the early 1900s, commemorates the last stand of the Sitka Indians by protecting and preserving remnants of their culture. Footpaths lead among the dense stands of hemlock, spruce, and alders. Within the forest stand authentic totems, some almost 60 feet tall.

Inside the Center, the arts and crafts section lets you watch Alaskan native artists at work. The building itself, constructed in Indian longhouse style, makes use of house poles from former potlatches (social gatherings).

Visitors are welcome at the Pioneers' Home where some aged Alaskan pioneers live. In front of the home a statue of "Skagway Bill" Fonda commemorates the old-timers who broke the early trails. A garden of native plants surrounds the building.

Sitka's big celebration is its Alaska Day Festival from October 16-18. There's a costume parade, re-enactment of the Transfer from Russia ceremony, Tlingit dances, and Baranof's Ball.

Juneau: a capital city

Perched on a narrow shelf between massive Mt. Juneau and the deep waters of Gastineau Channel sits Juneau, Alaska's capital. The town is, necessarily, long and rather narrow. Its streets twist and turn up the steep hillsides. In many places wooden staircases take up where streets leave off.

At first glance, Juneau's new skyscrapers make it appear very modern. But when you are wandering around the narrow downtown streets, take a look at some of the older buildings and glance up at weathered hillside perches. It's easy to see that much of the original flavor remains.

A look at history

In 1880 gold was discovered at Juneau. With the development of mining there, Juneau became an active center. Between 1900 and 1906, when Alaska was made the "District of Alaska," the capital was moved from Sitka to Juneau.

(Continued on page 35)

New Archangel *Russian Dancers perform colorful Cossack numbers to greet ships arriving in Sitka.*

Islands *dot Sitka's harbor. Snow-tipped Mt. Edgecumbe resembles Japan's Mt. Fujiyama.*

Shopping for native crafts

Many of Alaska's special crafts tell a story about life in the "Great Land." Gold nugget jewelry takes you back to the rush of '98. The art of working with jade, ivory, and soapstone has been handed down over countless years. Delicate baskets, ornamental beading, and forbidding masks speak of an ancient heritage.

The state provides a bounty of natural treasures: parkas, mukluks, furs, and skins come from its furry creatures; fresh seafood, including salmon and king crab, is canned or frozen; and a wealth of berries is preserved for take-home tasting.

One of the rarest gifts is an item made from qiviut (ki-vee-ute), the underwool of the musk ox. Every spring musk oxen lose their soft underwool. After it is plucked from the animal, it is sent to a spinning mill, returning as yarn. Natives knit the qiviut into soft scarves, stoles, caps, tunics, and sweaters. Qiviut is a rare treasure—and you pay a high price if you can find an item made of it.

Alaskan coral, generally retrieved from the icy waters around Kodiak, is processed in Hawaii and returned to Alaska for gem setting. Much of the polished coral ripples and shimmers like tiger's eye.

Wood carving has undergone a renaissance. Natives are again carving authentic totem poles, masks, panels, and screens. But beware: read up on totem designs or you may take home a cheap wood whittling.

Authentic Alaskan native art carries a Silver Hand emblem, guaranteeing that the articles you buy are made in Alaska by Alaskan natives who are at least one-quarter Eskimo, Aleut, or Indian.

Museums and native art co-ops show the best of craft selections. Look around before you start indiscriminate shopping.

Below is a listing of basic materials used by Alaskan craftsmen. You'll find good design examples throughout the state:

Ivory. As ivory becomes increasingly rare, prices go up. Fossil ivory is highly prized, having been taken from mastodon and ancient walrus unearthed from perpetually frozen ground. Scrimshaw—etching on ivory brought out by dyes—is found on bracelets, pendants, and earrings. Other ivory pieces include cribbage boards, billikens, and actual whale teeth and walrus tusks.

Baskets. Indian, Aleut, and Eskimo cultures each have distinctive baskets. Most are made of cedar or spruce. Techniques differ. Thin strips of cedar are woven after being peeled from the tree; spruce must be steamed and split into long fibers. The tighter the weave and the more intricate the work, the more expensive the piece. Cedar baskets are good buys in Southeast Alaska.

In the Arctic you may find a few examples of the baleen basket, made from interlocking whales' teeth. These are usually museum pieces.

Wood. Totems are made by carving wood. These magnificent and renowned forms of sculpture do not depict Indian gods; rather, they tell stories using symbolic birds, and fish. In early villages, animals represented certain families. Heraldic totem poles identified owners of abodes and the social status of chiefs and heads of houses. Other totems memorialized deceased chiefs or served as mortuary poles. Or they commemorated a "potlatch" (social get-together), in which competitive carvings vied for renown.

Wooden masks represent totem animals and supernatural or legendary characters. These were used in ceremonial dances and medicine men's healing rites.

Looking carefully, you might find carvings on instruments used for hunting, fishing, cooking, or even on the handles of the carving tools themselves, turning functional equipment into works of art.

Skin and fur. Due to the demands of severe weather and scarcity of materials, Eskimos perfected the art of utilizing animal fur and skin. Best buys are parkas, mukluks, and gloves. Hats and coats, though less expensive than in the "Lower 48," are still costly.

Bone. Artistic use of bone is another example of the native's waste-not ingenuity. Gigantic whale bones are used for making drying racks and skin boats; vertebrae form interesting mask designs, and discs may be used as bases for ivory carving.

Stone. Soapstone, oddly enough, is usually imported from outside Alaska and then crafted by natives. Smooth form and detail mark fine pieces. Green serpentine, the most popular and most easily shaped, is distributed by the government each summer to outlying villages.

Gold. Gold nugget jewelry is often a traveler's Alaskan souvenir. Look for a label guaranteeing that the nugget is genuine. Gold nugget jewelry is found throughout Alaska but prices are probably better in Fairbanks or Nome than anywhere else.

Jade. Centered in the Kobuk River area, north of the Arctic Circle, jade carving is a newer art form. Jade is primarily made into jewelry—but you can also find jade statuary, bookends, and other larger items.

Painting. Painting is a newcomer to Alaskan art. Natives working in this medium often paint stark and powerful scenes of life a century ago. More recent artists find the overwhelming views a source of inspiration.

One artist paints detailed weeds and flowers of the state; another works in soft sepia. Homer is an artists' colony; you'll also see good examples of art in Anchorage.

Clothing. The Eskimo woman's summer wrap is a colorful Paisley parka, usually handmade. You can occasionally find one for sale in an Eskimo shop or in the Arctic.

In Anchorage, some distinctive parkas in a "California weight" make excellent reminders of your northern visit.

A store in Juneau makes leather coats, jackets, hats, and purses by a patented process that eliminates sewing.

A Ketchikan shop offers fine silk screening on clothing, following traditional Indian designs. Along with your item, you receive a description of the animal clan.

Carved wooden masks—*originally worn in ceremonial dances and healing rites—seem to stare inquiringly at shoppers.*

...Continued from page 30

The Alaska-Juneau Gold Mining Company mill, which burned in 1964, remains a skeleton on the mountainside behind Juneau. It looks like a huge monument to the mining era. The mill has not operated since it was closed in 1941.

Across the channel is Douglas Island, site of the famous Treadwell gold mine, among others. The mines were closed down by a combination of floods, fires, a cave-in, and, in some cases, depletion. Today a bridge connects Juneau with the island and the city of Douglas.

Federal and state government payrolls, along with some fishing and lumbering, now form the basis for local business. In the last election, though, voters approved shifting the capital from Juneau to Willow (between Anchorage and Fairbanks). A terrible blow to Juneau and to all of Southeast Alaska, this move is being fought. It will take several years to resolve the issue.

Food and lodging

Accommodations in Juneau are the most extensive in Southeast Alaska. Your choice ranges from motels to new hotels to more venerable establishments with gold rush trappings. On the Mendenhall Loop Road, a large campground offers facilities for trailers and a spectacular view. There's a smaller campground in the Auke Bay region.

Meals range from standard fare in moderately priced coffee shops to expensive, intimate, candlelit suppers. Waterfront restaurants offer views of the active harbor. Juneau probably offers the most live entertainment and dancing of all the Panhandle towns.

Downtown attractions

Downtown Juneau can be best covered on a walking tour. Get a free guide and information sheet from the Visitor's Center, diagonally opposite the Baranof Hotel on Franklin Street. Total walking time is approximately 1½ hours.

American Sightseeing and Gray Line of Juneau offer city excursions in conjunction with their trip to Mendenhall Glacier (see page 36). They give you a chance to quickly locate points of interest you'll want to go back and visit more extensively. Here are several "musts" on your list:

The House of Wickersham houses one of the state's largest private collections of Alaskana. It's truly a living museum. Ruth Allman, niece of

Judge Wickersham (one of Alaska's pioneer legislators), explains mementos, relates tales of the judge's extensive travels, and—as a bonus—invites you to sit down and join her for coffee and a flaming sourdough waffle prepared at your table. You can get tickets for a house visit aboard your cruise ship or make reservations at the Gray Line and Alaska Tour & Marketing Services desks in the Baranof Hotel.

The Alaska State Museum is another important Juneau highlight. It contains an outstanding collection of Tlingit, Haida, Athabascan, Aleut, and Eskimo artifacts, historical exhibits, unique Alaskana, and a section featuring plant and animal life. A rotating gallery on the main floor features a monthly new art exhibit. The museum is open seven days a week from 9 a.m. to 5 p.m. weekdays, 1 to 5 p.m. weekends, and during evenings in summer.

On the lighter side is the Red Dog Saloon, still maintaining its old-time dance hall aura with sawdust-covered floor, honky tonk piano, and community singing, and a Gold Rush Minstrel Show at the Baranof Hotel.

Down at Last Chance Basin, site of a once-flourishing gold mine, enjoy a salmon bake nightly, rain or shine, from June through mid-September. Music and song accompany dinner. Visit the Mining Museum and Opera House for a theatrical performance. Advance tickets are required.

Visitors can also tour a mine on the Gold Panning and Gold Mine Tour. In addition to learning of the history of the mine, you'll get a chance to pan in Gold Creek, site of the original discovery.

Of further interest in the city is St. Nicholas Russian Orthodox Church, the Four Story Totem, Alaska State Capitol Building, Juneau

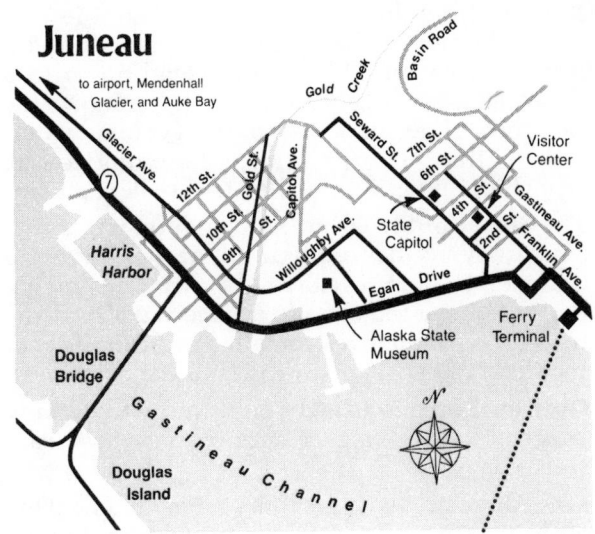

Guests share Alaskan lore and flaming sourdough at House of Wickersham.

Memorial Library and Totem, Governor's Mansion (not open for tours), Gold Creek, and the State Office Building (contains Old Witch Totem and Alaska's first theater organ, restored for free Friday noontime concerts). On the third floor of the Federal Building you can see a native crafts exhibit of Indians, Aleuts, and Eskimos, open 8 a.m. to 5 p.m. weekdays.

Shopping

Juneau shops carry handicrafts from all over the state: Eskimo walrus ivory carvings (jewelry, cribbage and chess sets), whimsical little Billikens (good luck charms carved from walrus tusks and teeth of sperm whales), Haida and Tlingit crafts, paintings by famous Alaskan artists, and rare Chilkat blankets.

Interesting shopping available in the city includes Nina's Originals, which sells unusual leather coats, jackets, hats, and purses made by a patented process that eliminates sewing. Alaska Native Arts and Crafts retail store specializes in authentic Indian and Eskimo handicrafts. Among other promising shops is a bookstore well-stocked with varied Alaskan titles.

Outside the city

Several side trips from Juneau produce surprising delights. Though roads don't reach out too far, Alaskans think nothing of taking off by boat or plane for a few hours, a day, or a weekend.

Mendenhall, Juneau's "drive-in" glacier, is a crowd-drawer. Sightseeing buses operate throughout the year from town. Included in the 2½-hour trip is a stop at the Chapel-by-the-Lake overlooking Auke Lake, probably one of Alaska's most photographed scenes. Nearby is the Juneau college campus.

Mendenhall Glacier (now retreating) lies just 13 miles from downtown Juneau. Here the U.S. Forest Service maintains an observatory and interpretive center. Hiking trails lead down to a closer look at the glacier's foot or up along the side through a rain forest, past a gushing waterfall, to fine view points for listening to the crunching and grinding of the never-silent glacier.

The Shrine of St. Terese, hidden in trees of a tiny causeway-connected island along Favorite Channel, is 23 miles north of Juneau. Following the stations of the cross to a large crucifix at the top of the island gives you a magnificent view of the Chilkat Range, many miles to the northwest.

Over on Douglas Island you'll find wide, sandy beaches for walking or sunning on those rare warm days.

From Juneau, many air tours are available. One of the most popular is the flight over the Juneau Icecap. High above the Gastineau Channel you'll see the communities of Douglas and Juneau, as well as the bulging expanse of the Juneau Icecap, which spawns all the glaciers in the area, including the Mendenhall.

Lynn Canal excursions are available in season from Juneau or Skagway via the M.V. Fairweather, a sightseeing boat. Price for the daylight cruise includes round-trip transportation, overnight accommodations, and dinner.

Several popular lodges can be reached by air from Juneau. Hood Bay and Thayer Lake lodges on Admiralty Island, 80 miles from Juneau, specialize in fishing and hiking.

You can charter a boat for fishing or photographic safaris along fiords populated by seals, whales, birds, and other wildlife.

A very special event during the last part of July or first part of August is the annual Golden North Salmon Derby. Everybody except babies and baby-sitters joins the fishing fun. Businesses fold up; signs on closed doors proclaim, "Gone Fishin'."

Juneau, along with other Southeast towns, celebrates Fourth of July in old-fashioned style, complete with fire engines and dancing.

Glacier Bay National Monument

About 100 miles northwest of Juneau in the Fairweather Range of the St. Elias Mountains is one of Alaska's most dramatic sites—Glacier Bay National Monument. In an area of 4,400 square miles spread more than 20 tremendous glaciers and many other impressive smaller ones.

Several tidewater glaciers offer a spectacular show of geologic forces in action. As water undermines ice fronts, great blocks of ice up to 200 feet high break loose and crash into the sea, creating huge waves and filling the narrow inlets with massive icebergs.

Muir and Johns Hopkins Glaciers discharge such great volumes of ice that it may be difficult to approach their cliffs too closely. Margerie Glacier, on Tarr Inlet, though also very active, is more accessible. From a safe distance of ½ mile, boaters can watch ice falling from the glacier face.

Two mountain ranges feed these ponderous rivers of ice. The Takhinsha Range, largely unexplored, feeds Muir Glacier and others on the east side of the bay. Glaciers on the west side have their origin in the lofty Fairweather range, which culminates in 15,300-foot Mt. Fairweather. The Grand Pacific Glacier, originating in Canada between the two ranges, is a product of both mountain systems.

When George Vancouver first visited in 1794, this region was all part of a massive icefield that filled the bay. Today, the ice has receded 65 miles to create the fiords of Glacier Bay.

Getting there

No roads reach Glacier Bay. Access is by scheduled jet service to Gustavus Airport from Juneau or air charter from Haines, Juneau, or Sitka. Cruise ships enter both arms of the bay for a day's visit. Most travelers choose a tour package from Juneau that includes air fare, lodging, and an excursion boat cruise.

Where to stay

Park headquarters is at Bartlett Cove. One of Alaska's most attractive wild country chalets, Glacier Bay Lodge has 55 units, a dining room, and a lounge for evening gatherings. It's open from mid-May to mid-September. For information and reservations, write to Glacier Bay Lodge, Suite 312, Park Place Bldg., Seattle, WA 98101.

Near the monument is Gustavus Inn, a pleasant homestead farmhouse on an active farm. A new, year-round fishing lodge may be in the planning stages. Bus transportation is available for the 10-mile trip to Bartlett Cove.

Ranger *invites you to feel the spongy texture of mosses that cover rocks in Glacier Bay National Monument.*

Shopper *beams with delight as she tries on jaunty sealskin parka—a very cozy souvenir from Juneau.*

What to do

Highlight of any Glacier Bay visit is a close look at the star performers—the glaciers themselves. A one-day excursion boat (lunch is not included in the fare) leaves Bartlett Cove daily during the summer. Park naturalists aboard explain glacial activity, call attention to wildlife, and point out how new growth begins on land left by glacial retreat.

Alternative packages from the lodge allow a visitor to stay overnight at the face of the glaciers.

Miles of beaches make camping a delight if you bring all your own equipment. (Also bring your own food if you do not plan to eat at the lodge.) A number of hiking trails cut through Bartlett Cove's luxuriant rain forests; park rangers conduct hikes and evening programs from the lodge.

Sometimes you'll spot mountain goats, spouting whales, or hair seals sleeping on icebergs. Plentiful halibut and salmon make this a great fishing area. Large numbers of waterfowl— loons, cormorants, geese, common eiders and other ducks, various gulls and shore birds, murrelets, guillemots, and puffins—wheel over the coves and inlets. Ravens, grouse, and eagles inhabit the shorelands.

In the summer bears are attracted to streams by the huge numbers of spawning salmon. At Bear Track Cove, the lumbering animals have worn trails along the stream banks.

Glacier Bay's climate is usually overcast (good for observing maximum color in glaciers) with one or two beautifully clear days. Watch for spectacular, hours-long sunsets.

For additional camping and hiking information, write to the Superintendent, Glacier Bay National Monument, Box 1089, Juneau, AK 99802.

Southeast's gateways to the Interior

From Haines, Port Chilkoot, and Skagway, it's easy to go farther into Alaska's interior. Regularly scheduled planes, trains, and ships make these terminals virtual beehives of activity. Although Haines and Skagway aren't connected by road, they're only a few minutes apart by plane or an hour's ride by ferry.

Haines and Port Chilkoot—ferry terminus

On the upper reaches of beautiful Lynn Canal, surrounded by high, snow-clad peaks, lie the side-by-side cities of Haines and Port Chilkoot. Visually, each has preserved strong traces of its original look.

Haines, a former fur trading post, became Haines Mission (Presbyterian) in 1881. Port Chilkoot (now incorporated by Haines) was originally established as Fort William H. Seward in 1903. Following World War II, it was sold to a group of war veterans. Though officers' quarters are now private homes, the fort architecture remains remarkably military. "Walk-about" tours of the fort, now a State and Federal Historical Site, are free.

Compared to towns in lower Southeast, Haines is a hub of transportation, reached by land, sea, and air. Cruise ships don't stop here, but ferries discharge both passengers and vehicles for the trek up splendid Haines Highway.

Prevailing industries are commercial fishing and lumbering. You might see a Japanese freighter being loaded with timber at the dock. Canneries operate from time to time; one of the most picturesque is out Mud Bay Road to Letnikoff Cove.

History of the Haines area is the history of the Chilkat Indians. Klukwan, which once had 65 houses and about 600 Indian residents, was the main settlement. Today only a few houses remain standing.

These early warlike and wily Indian traders dominated commerce with the Athabascans in the interior until the invasion of the fur traders and the gold-seekers, who used the Dalton trail route to the Klondike.

Accomplished in arts and crafts, the Chilkats were working copper when the first white men arrived. The tribe excelled in making colorful goat hair blankets, still used in Tlingit ceremonials.

Lodging in Haines is limited to a couple of downtown motels and the 1900-era Halsingland Hotel in Port Chilkoot. Forming one side of the old fort's parade ground, the spacious hotel offers good food. Nearby is a pleasant camping area and trailer court. You'll also find other campgrounds near town and along the Haines Highway.

One highlight at Port Chilkoot is the display of ancient arts, crafts, music, and dances of the Chilkat tribe. This revival of interest was stimulated by Alaska Indian Arts, Inc., a nonprofit organization. An authentic Indian tribal house, totems, and other replicas of Indian life have been built.

When ferries are in port, young Chilkat Dancers in full regalia perform colorful dances of the northwest coast Indians. You can buy carved totems, masks, and other Chilkat craft products at the Totem Workshop of Alaska Indian Arts, Inc. Guided tours show artisans at work.

Other attractions in the area include Paradise

Ship passengers *line rails for close look at active Margerie Glacier in Glacier Bay National Monument.*

Glacier Bay Lodge *rooftop soars above surrounding rain forest on Bartlett Cove.*

THE PANHANDLE **39**

Cove, picturesque fish canneries, strawberry farms, and the base of the old Dalton Trail.

Naturalists come to Haines because the area has one of North America's largest concentrations of bald eagles. October and November are particularly good times to observe these eagles when they feed on late-run spawning salmon.

From Flat Bay Road, you'll get a good view of Rainbow and Davidson glaciers (Rainbow is a hanging glacier).

Next door to the Customs and Immigration Office in Haines is a Visitor Information Center.

Some special events: May salmon derby; Haines Dalton Trail Days in July with old-time costumes, parade, midway, and dances; and the Southeast Alaska State Fair in August.

The Haines Highway takes off from Haines, heading up to meet the Alaska Highway 159 miles north. Not far from Haines, along the highway, are the ghost town of Porcupine and the Klukwan Indian village—one of the oldest native settlements of the region and seat of ancient Tlingit culture.

Skagway—the last frontier

Wedged in between mountain ranges at the far end of Lynn Canal, Skagway looks like a movie back lot for a forthcoming Western. Its gravel streets, board sidewalks, and false-front buildings make you feel that you're stepping back in time.

There is little rush and push in Skagway today. The town is small. The 20,000 population it had during its heyday has dwindled to a mere 750 residents. But those who are left take time to be friendly, and Skagway offers a revealing look into Alaska's past.

Skagway's history started at the time of the Klondike gold rush of 1897. It was the starting point for two main trails to the gold fields—one that led from Skagway through Dyea and onto the famous Trail of '98 over Chilkoot Pass, and the other the White Pass Trail, a route you can follow today on the White Pass & Yukon Railway.

Skagway boomed with turbulent history under the gang rule of "Soapy" Smith—until Soapy was shot by a vigilante. Performances depicting the life and times of this infamous character are timed for cruise ship and ferry arrivals.

Lodging is quite adequate. It includes small motels, a restored and renovated gold rush era hotel, and a large hotel decorated in plush, turn-of-the-century decor. Hotels have restaurants, and you'll find a couple of small coffee shops on the main street.

Trailer parks come and go in Skagway, but you're sure to find a small campground a few miles out of town on the Skagway River. The town's store will supply your grocery needs.

Night life is restricted to nights when ships are in port. Then you can watch local home talent in the "Days of '98" show—gambling games with fake money, dancing, skits, and the re-enactment of the "Shooting of Dan McGrew." You can also enjoy a dramatic presentation of the Mighty Moose Melodrama, held at present in a tent along the street, or "Soapy Lives" at the Arctic Brotherhood Hall.

The Klondike Gold Rush National Historical Park preserves most of downtown Skagway, the routes over the passes, and even reaches south to Seattle to include Pioneer Square, the jumping-off spot for the Alaskan gold rush. This unusual historical park was dedicated in 1977 to memorialize the agony and glory of the gold rush days. An interpretive center is planned for the railroad depot at the foot of Broadway Street.

Skagway's city museum, housed in Alaska's first granite building, contains many relics of those days of '98. Opened originally as a Methodist college in 1899, the building later became a U.S. District Court of Alaska. Many of the old court records are on display, along with some of the old courtroom furnishings.

(Continued on page 43)

Visitors *watch totem carving; you can buy poles, other native carvings throughout Southeastern Alaska.*

Trek to Dawson City

Of all Yukon Territory attractions, Canada's Klondike gold fields are the best known. Historic Dawson City brings back to life the romantic days of the Klondike gold rush. Many of the original buildings still stand, intriguing visitors with their "Trail of '98" history.

North of Whitehorse, a good gravel road branches north to Dawson City. It rejoins the Alaska Highway 510 miles later at Tetlin Junction on the Alaska side of the border.

Accommodations, food, and gasoline are available on the Klondike Highway at Carmacks, Pelly Crossing, and Mayo. At Pelly Crossing a daily riverboat tour takes sightseers to the ghost town of Ft. Selkirk where the Hudson's Bay Company started the first Yukon trading post in 1847.

Dawson City, once a rich and bawdy gold rush town, was, in its heyday, the largest settlement north of San Francisco and west of Winnipeg.

Yukon history is peppered with colorful characters, many of whom lived in Dawson City. Klondike Kate (whose real name was Kitty Rockwell) came to Dawson as a dance hall girl and became the toast of the Klondike. Arizona Charlie Meadows, a veteran of the Buffalo Bill show, sold whiskey to miners until he lost his bar in a flood and was forced to resort to sharp shooting to make a living. Three of the main figures of the gold discovery—Tagish Charley, Skookum Jim, and Kate Carmack—are laid to rest in a small cemetery 50 miles south of Whitehorse on the northern shores of Lake Bennett.

After the gold rush, Dawson City gradually became a virtual ghost town, reviving only after the road from Whitehorse was completed. Today, Dawson City is primarily a summer tourist town, although some mining continues.

In summer, you can still hear strains of honky-tonk music punctuated by the click of roulette wheels. The city revives the past and invites visitors to participate.

Now a historical complex, Dawson City is being restored by the Canadian government. Its big celebration is Discovery Day, held the third weekend in August.

Other attractions include miniature sternwheeler cruises, rafting trips on the Yukon or other rivers, "mellerdrammers" in the restored Palace Grand Theatre, gambling and cancan shows at Diamond Tooth Gertie's, touring the *S.S. Keno* (last steamer on the Yukon River), and visits to Robert Service and Jack London cabins. Gold rush films are shown daily in historic St. Paul's Anglican Church.

A stroll along the boardwalks takes you by restored residences, shops, and museums. Several mines permit you to pan your own "color."

From Dawson City to the border, you might meet ore trucks coming off side roads with a tendency to highball. Drivers are advised to pull over and let them pass.

Near the border is the Boundary Roadhouse (cabins, limited trailer space, gas, and home cooking). A branch road goes to Eagle, on the banks of the Yukon, where Judge James Wickersham established the first U.S. Court in the interior. You can see remains of old Ft. Egbert.

After crossing the border, you head southwest on the Taylor Highway to Tetlin Junction. The road follows the high country, through a wilderness with scant population. Portions of this highway are closed in the winter. The main stopping place is a lodge near Fortymile River (service station, good food, friendly bar). Some gold mining still goes on in this district.

The Taylor Highway joins the Alaska Highway at Mile 1301, Tetlin Junction, where you'll find Forty-Mile Roadhouse with all facilities.

Chilkat Dancers *from Haines, authentically garbed, re-enact ancient Indian lore to music.*

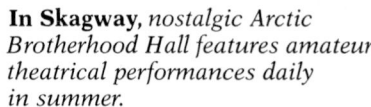

In Skagway, *nostalgic Arctic Brotherhood Hall features amateur theatrical performances daily in summer.*

...*Continued from page 40*

At Gold Rush Cemetery, north of town, you can see the grave of Frank Reid, who was gunned down by Soapy in a shootout after a public meeting held to rid the town of lawless Mr. Smith. Many other graves testify to lost hopes of those attempting to make their fortune. Just beyond the cemetery is an intriguing hike to Reid's Falls.

Annual events of note are the Fourth of July celebration and the "Sourdough Days" on Labor Day weekend.

From Skagway you can take a short sightseeing flight to Haines and Port Chilkoot or a longer flight over the ice fields of Glacier Bay.

The much-wanted Skagway to Carcross and Whitehorse Highway was recently completed and is now open to traffic. There are several other view points to drive to, though little is left of the ghost town of Dyea. Scheduled excursions give you a good tour, tell tales of the town's lusty past, and leave you time for shopping.

Several gift shops, such as Kirmse's (one of the oldest in town) offer opportunities for browsing and buying. At Kirmse's the largest and smallest gold nugget chains may be seen. The largest weighs 3 pounds and is worth several thousand dollars; the smallest is made of 283 tiny gold nuggets.

Corrington's "bike-and-dog" runs through town lead visitors to a shop specializing in good native art. Of particular interest is the collection of Arctic ivory pieces.

The White Pass & Yukon Railway

A narrow-gauge route to Whitehorse follows the trail of the '98ers over the Coast Mountains. Before the railroad was completed in 1900, some 60,000 men fought their way on foot across infamous White Pass to the gold fields of the Klondike.

Building a railroad through the rugged St. Elias Mountains which separate the Yukon from the sea was quite a challenge. On hand to tackle it was Michael J. Heney, known as the "Irish Prince." Heney met in Skagway with Sir Thomas Tancrede, who represented an English group willing to finance a railway. After an all-night discussion, the construction of a route through the toughest railroad country in North America was no longer a dream, but soon to be a reality.

Materials arrived at Skagway on May 27, 1898, and soon ribbons of steel pointed north towards the White Pass. By July, a passenger train operated a distance of 4 miles, the first train to run in Alaska and the only railway so far north in North America at that time.

Track reached the summit in February of 1899 and, by July, construction reached Lake Bennett in British Columbia. While gangs blasted and hacked their way through the pass from the south, construction started from Whitehorse toward Carcross. The two groups met at Carcross on July 29, 1900, completing the construction of one of the most difficult railroads ever engineered.

Today you relax in coach chairs and follow what was once a difficult foot trail in comfort and safety. When you board the train, you receive a descriptive brochure keyed to regularly marked mileposts that point out spots of special historic and scenic interest along the 111-mile route.

The railroad makes connections throughout the year with state ferries at Skagway. If you wish, you can transport your car by flatcar from Skagway to Whitehorse, on the Alaska Highway. Allow a full day for the one-way trip between Skagway and Whitehorse and another day to return. During the summer, the railway operates a one-day, round-trip tour (featuring a trencherman's lunch) to Lake Bennett, a mountain-framed mirror of deep blue water reflecting snow-capped peaks.

Sitting on the left side of the train (heading north) will allow you more panoramic views over the pass. Photographers are permitted to step out on platforms to get photos. The most spectacular views occur from Skagway to Lake Bennett.

Sights along the way, between Skagway and Whitehorse, include Tunnel Mountain. Probably no tunnel in the world was built under greater difficulties than this one; it had to penetrate a perpendicular barrier of rock which juts out of the mountainside like a giant flying buttress. Machinery and equipment to construct this 250-foot tunnel were manhandled up the sides of cliffs.

A short distance from the summit of the pass, a deep canyon is spanned by a steel cantilever bridge, 215 feet above the creek's bed. Below in Dead Horse Gulch (named for the 3,000 pack animals that plunged to their death here), winds the White Pass Trail.

White Pass summit, elevation 2,900 feet, marks the international boundary between the U.S. and Canada.

At Lake Bennett, your luncheon stop, you have time to walk to the old log church on the hill, built by the sourdoughs in 1898. It was at Lake Bennett that the stampeders paused to build rafts and boats to carry themselves and their equipment through Bennett, Tagish, and Marsh lakes to the Yukon River and on to the Klondike.

Carcross, at the north end of Lake Bennett, was formerly named Caribou Crossing because of the great herds which once crossed this natural ford.

Canadian customs and immigration are located here.

Hiking the Chilkoot Pass

For the past several years, nearly a thousand people each year have hiked the famous gold rush trail from Dyea over Chilkoot Pass and down to the headwaters of the Yukon River in British Columbia. Not since the winter of 1897-98, when thousands of fortune seekers poured over this and nearby White Pass on their way to Klondike gold fields, have so many made the crossing on foot.

The White Pass & Yukon Railway whisks passengers over White Pass, but the Chilkoot, still wild and undeveloped, is for foot travelers only. It provides an opportunity to see the country almost as the miners saw it nearly a century ago.

The resurgence of activity along the 32-mile trail began when the state marked and cleared the way to its summit, bridged streams, and constructed a couple of log cabins for hikers.

The hike begins 9 miles northwest of Skagway at Dyea. The trail follows the Taiya River to its source near Chilkoot Pass, crossing the stream several times. You walk through a coastal rain forest, occasionally over boardwalks that traverse bogs where trillium and devil's club mingle with fireweed and sword ferns in the shade of towering hemlocks.

Don't be misled by those famous and intimidating photographs of heavily burdened miners struggling up steep slopes toward the summit of 3,739-foot Chilkoot Pass. Most of the trail is easy going, and you gain only a thousand feet over the first 13 miles to Sheep Camp.

But then you begin to climb in earnest, gaining 2,700 feet in 3 miles to the summit. The final quarter mile is practically an all-fours ascent over talus—but, once at the top, hikers are rewarded with broad, majestic views of glacial peaks. Wildlife is abundant: you may see Alaskan brown bear, mountain goat, moose, ptarmigan, or porcupine.

The Canadian section of trail descends slowly from the pass into dry, open country studded with dwarf spruce and pine, past several pristine lakes and ponds to Bennett Lake. Once miners built boats here and floated more than 500 miles down the Yukon River to Dawson City. Today, at Bennett, you can board the train, which makes daily afternoon trips back to Skagway.

The Klondike miners were notorious litterbugs. Along the trail—often called the longest museum in America—you'll see dilapidated cabins, abandoned cookstoves, boots, horseshoes, telephone wire, boats, sleds, bottles, and other debris. These discarded items are considered artifacts today and should remain undisturbed.

If you want to avoid transporting backpacking gear to Alaska, guides will equip and lead you over the route in 4½ days. All you need to bring is warm clothing, rain gear, and hiking boots.

The White Pass & Yukon Railroad *whisks you over the spectacular Coast Mountains; if you prefer, you can follow the famous gold rush trail on foot.*

The guide will supply food, tents, backpacks, sleeping bags, and wilderness know-how.

Such an adventure is strictly for the visitor who has plenty of time on his schedule of touring Alaska. It is included in no group excursions. Check in Juneau for qualified guides.

Backpackers roughing it on their own should carry a topographic map; they should also come prepared for wet weather on the south side of the pass and possible freezing temperatures at night. Summer is the only time to attempt the climb; the season usually ends around mid-September.

Two winter rendezvous

One sure way to break up the winter doldrums in the north is to have a festival. Two of the biggest and best take place in February—Anchorage's "Rondy" and the Sourdough Rendezvous in Whitehorse, capital of the Yukon. Many visitors come from the Outside to join the revels of these lighthearted events.

In Whitehorse

A parade along the city streets launches the Yukon Sourdough Rendezvous. Cancan dancers and businessmen with scruffy beards wend their way through saloons and dance halls. At fun-filled Frantic Follies, the local vaudeville show, a troupe performs song-and-dance revues. Highlighting the festival are recitations from the works of Robert Service, often called the Bard of the Klondike.

Among outdoor sporting events are dog sled races, bed races, a tug of war, flour-packing (the Yukon version of weight-lifting), and a whipsaw competition.

Fiddlers fill the air with music for some fine, old-fashioned foot-stomping. To top everything off, be sure to get a taste of savory moose stew during this three to four-day celebration.

In Anchorage

The Anchorage Fur Rendezvous grows more exciting (and lasts longer) every year. "Rondy" features more than 100 planned events, along with many rather spontaneous happenings.

Called the "Mardi Gras of the North," the Rendezvous dates back to the 1930s when it began as a down-to-earth fur auction. Trappers brought their pelts to town and sold them to buyers from around the world. The auction, still active today, attracts fashion

buyers—and also enables visitors to purchase furs at very attractive prices.

The favorite feature is the dog-mushing event of the year—the World Championship Sled Dog Race. Mushers come from all over Alaska and the "Lower 48."

You'll also encounter gambling, a Miners and Trappers Ball, and an annual parade. Arts and crafts shows are sprinkled through the scene. Sports events include cross-country skiing, snowmobile races, wrist wrestling, and sky diving.

During the 10-day festival tourists spend more than $1 million. It's no wonder "Rondy" grows each year.

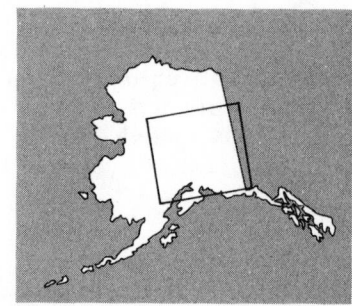

Into the Interior

North of the Coastal Range and east of the Alaska Range lies the part of Alaska usually referred to as "the Interior," a great region of broad river valleys, muskeg flats, and old, worn-down mountains.

The Russians and British penetrated this region between 1834 and 1847 through waterways in summer and along dog trails in winter. In 1883 and 1885, some years after the United States purchased Alaska, the U.S. Army's Lt. Frederick Schwatka and Lt. Henry T. Allen made expeditions into this wild area. Allen went in by the Copper River, where he reported there were great ore deposits.

Discovery of gold on Fortymile River in 1886 lured prospectors and miners a decade before the more fabled Klondike rush. When another discovery was made in 1895 on Birch Creek near Circle City, that town boomed to 500 population. Then the Dawson rush of 1896 drew the miners.

Fairbanks, Alaska's second largest city and the heart of the interior, calls itself the Golden Heart of Alaska. And so it was—until the late 1930s—when gold became scarcer and dwindled in value.

Some thirty years later, Fairbanks again became the center of a new rush—this time for "black gold." As a take-off point for the North Slope oil fields, the city is again a boom town. Even gold is making a slight comeback. You can see working mines and a giant dredge in operation.

Exploring the Interior

You can reach Fairbanks, center of inland Alaska, by air, rail, or highway. With several thousand miles of road to travel, many visitors either drive up the Alaska Highway or rent a car in Fairbanks to penetrate the interior at their own pace.

Sightseeing excursions reach into the interior by motor coach from Whitehorse or Anchorage and air flights from Anchorage or Arctic cities.

Getting there by rail or air

Northwest Orient Airlines flies to Fairbanks from Seattle and Portland. Alaska Airlines operates from Seattle to Fairbanks. Wien Air Alaska and Alaska Airlines fly direct from Anchorage to Fairbanks. Wien also serves Fairbanks from Juneau via Whitehorse and from other Alaskan towns.

Alaska Railroad operates an all-day trip between Anchorage, Denali National Park, and Fairbanks. Dining and lounge cars add to the appeal of this attractive travel alternative.

Along the Alaska Highway

The Alaska Highway begins officially in Dawson Creek, B.C.—a booming, bustling town in the rich agricultural and oil country of the Peace River. People enjoy having their picture taken at the popular "Mile 0" post that marks the start of the 1,523-mile highway.

Most of the Alaska Highway is in Canada. Basically a good gravel road, the highway is paved for a short distance out of Dawson Creek and from the Alaska border into Fairbanks. Read page 19 for driving tips.

You'll travel 300 miles from Dawson Creek to Fort Nelson, another boom town, near the site of an early Hudson's Bay Trading Post. From there it's another 618 miles to Whitehorse. (When you arrive at Morley River, you'll be about halfway to Fairbanks.)

Whitehorse, Yukon. Whitehorse is the governmental and trading center for Yukon Territory. Once the focal point of navigation on the

Reflection of Mt. McKinley's snow-shrouded summit ripples on face of nearby tundra pond.

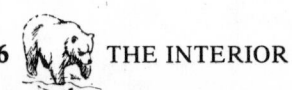

The Interior

Circle City—end of road to hot springs and unobstructed views of midnight sun

Dawson City, Y.T.—Klondike miners' goal

August Discovery Day celebration
Diamond Tooth Gertie's cancan show
Palace Grand Theatre "mellerdrammer"
Robert Service and Jack London cabins
Yukon River rafting

Fairbanks—gold and oil boom town

Alaskaland's collection of history
Discovery sternwheeler cruise
Pipeline visit
University of Alaska Museum

Mt. McKinley National Park—wildlife preserve

Back country hiking and camping
Park bus tour
Views of mammoth Mt. McKinley

Nenana—scene of state's largest lottery —guessing when spring "break-up" will happen on Tanana River

Whitehorse, Y.T.—terminus of White Pass & Yukon Railway

"Frantic Follies" variety show
Klondike sternwheeler museum
McBride Museum
Riverboat cruise

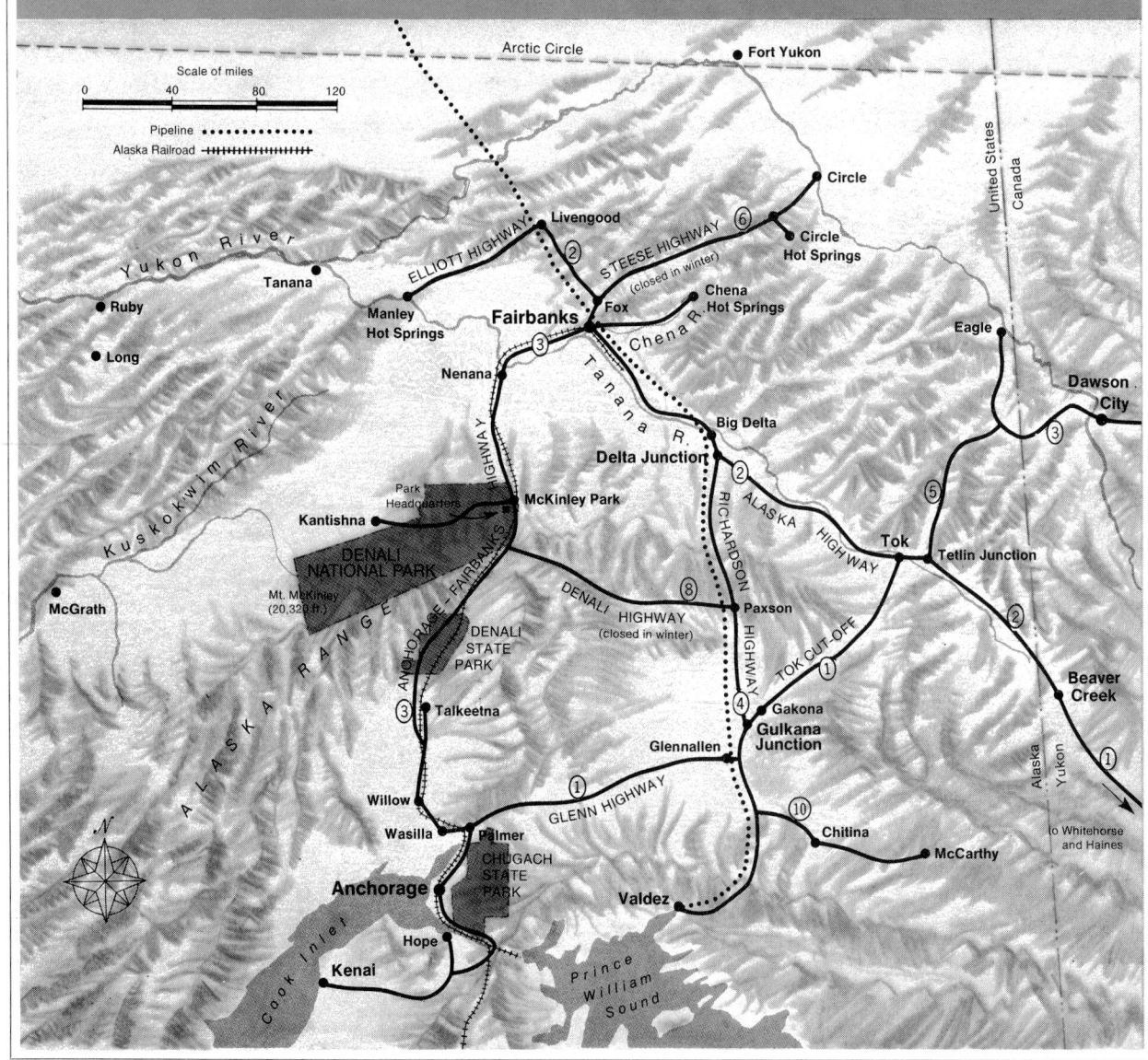

Yukon River, the city has preserved one of the fleet of 250 riverboats that plied local waters during the days of the gold rush. The *S.S. Klondike*, an old sternwheel steamer-turned-museum, is beached on the river banks. Board the craft—now a National Historical Site—for a tour.

Be sure to visit the MacBride Museum with its fine collection from the Yukon's past. Inside the sod-roofed building you'll see an outstanding collection of relics and photographs from the gold rush and riverboat era. Outside displays include exhibits of railway and mining equipment as well as Sam McGee's Cabin.

Another place in Whitehorse where history comes alive is Old Log Church Museum. Built in 1900 as an Anglican church, it had among its parishioners the famous Yukoner Robert W. Service. It was for a church concert in 1904 that the well-known poet composed the ballad of "Dangerous Dan McGrew." He never recited it there, however, because the parishioners felt it was too risque.

He went on to write other poems of the Yukon, and in 1908, when he moved to Dawson, they were published in a collection called *Songs of a Sourdough.*

Informal mini-trips take visitors through the city to historic Lake Laberge, or upstream to the hydroelectric dam at Schwatka Lake. The water backed up by the dam forms the lake which tamed the infamous Whitehorse Rapids where author Jack London earned a small fortune piloting riverboats.

On the east side of the dam is one of the world's longest all-wooden fish ladders. In August, when salmon are running upstream to spawn, visitors can view the fish through a window at the side of the ladder.

If you're staying overnight in Whitehorse, you might want to include an evening's entertainment at the "Frantic Follies" vaudeville show.

From Whitehorse, you can catch the White Pass & Yukon Railway to Skagway. You might also take a river cruise through Miles Canyon on the *M/V Schwatka.* A suspension bridge across the 125-foot-deep canyon can be reached by side road from the Alaska Highway.

The path to the right leads to the site of Canyon City where stampeders portaged freight around the rapids on a horse-drawn tramline. You can still see remains of old cabins and of the tramline itself.

Circle to Dawson City. North of Whitehorse, a good gravel road branches north to Dawson City, Canada—a delightful historical remnant of the romantic Klondike days. From Dawson City you can rejoin the Alaska Highway at Tetlin Junction, Alaska.

Dawson City offers plenty for the visitor to see and do. Probably the most interesting activity is a get-acquainted stroll up and down the old wooden sidewalks where you'll mingle with the spirits of Coatless Curley, Hamgrease Jimmy, Diamond Tooth Gertie, and Nellie the Pig.

Now a historical complex, Dawson City is being restored. Many of the old shrines have received face-lifting and it's business as usual at some long-time firms.

At the Dawson City Visitor Information Centre (5th Ave. and Queen St.), open daily during summer, you can get information on city sightseeing tours, Yukon River tours, Klondike River float trips, and evening entertainment. Dawson City is Canada's only licensed gambling city.

For additional information, see the Dawson City Special Feature on page 41.

Whitehorse to Tok. Beyond Whitehorse you travel through scenic country past log structures built by early prospectors. About 76 miles north is the Aishihik Road (open summer only). Heading 17 miles down this road, you reach Otter Falls. Here are provided picnic sites, a public campground, and a boat launch on Aishihik Lake.

The Alaska Highway leads next to Haines Junction, headquarters for the Kluane National Park. The park is bordered by the Alaska Highway and the Haines Highway that branches south to connect with the Alaska state ferry system at the top of the Inside Passage.

Continuing on beyond Haines Junction, you skirt resplendent Kluane Lake. At Mile 1202 (Beaver Creek) are Canadian customs and immigration and a customary stop—the Alas/Kon Border Lodge (136 rooms, dining room, cocktail lounge, service station).

At Tok, where the paved Glenn Highway from Anchorage joins the Alaska Highway, a visitors center and museum awaits you. Though a comparatively small settlement, Tok offers a number of places to stay, including an exclusive campground in town and a public campground, Moon Lake, 18 miles out of town.

Tok residents raise, breed, and train dogs. The village is one of Alaska's headquarters for dog mushing, a state sport. Tok also acts as a trading center for several Athabascan Indian villages. Good buys are birch baskets, beaded moccasins, boots, and necklaces.

Tok to Fairbanks. From Tok the Alaska Highway follows the Tanana River drainage to Delta Junction, where it converges with the Richardson Highway. A strung-out city along the Delta River, Delta Junction possesses boom town characteristics because of the Alaska pipeline construction. The pipeline crosses over the Tanana River near Delta Junction.

In 1926 a small herd of bison was placed in the Delta area. They have thrived and multiplied to the point where homesteaders—and motorists—regard them as a nuisance. A salt lick on the far side of the Delta River is an attempt to keep the bison contained.

At Delta you are 98 miles from Fairbanks. As you drive, keep your eyes alert for moose feeding in swamps along the road. You'll enjoy some worthwhile view turnouts along the highway. Richardson Roadhouse, Hollies Motel and Cafe, and Aurora Lodge offer meals and accommodations. At Salcha River (good fishing) and at Quartz and Harding lakes you'll find campgrounds.

Fourteen miles from Fairbanks is the community of North Pole. You can visit Santa Claus House, a gift shop, and a post office.

Seven miles from Fairbanks, the Eskimo Museum contains authentic Alaskan souvenirs and museum pieces.

Travelers who drive the complete Alaska Highway to its official end at the sod-roofed log cabin visitor's center on the bank of the Chena River have earned their feeling of accomplishment. A sign proclaims they have covered 1,523 miles from Mile 0 at Dawson Creek, B.C. (700 miles north of the U.S. border).

Fairbanks – a boom town

Fairbanks is a flat city. Distinguished only by the water flowing around its northwestern edge, the city initially disappoints many travelers. From a plane, though, you can see low, rolling hills of birch and white spruce. To the north and south, the towering mountains begin.

Because of its location as a service and supply point for the pipeline, Fairbanks has grown rapidly in a somewhat disorganized fashion. The city is loaded with contrasts—fancy new homes, hotels, and shopping centers next door to creaky log cabins and buildings dating from the early 1900s.

Expect dramatic climate changes. Winter temperatures can drop to −60°F; summer weather can climb to 90°F. Daylight hours are long—about 21 hours—and it never really gets dark in June and July. Though rain is scarce, you can expect sudden, brief showers.

A touch of history

Fairbanks got its start in 1901 when Captain E. T. Barnette, a trader and riverboat operator, was sidetracked into the Chena River on his way up the Tanana. When Felix Pedro, a prospector, told him about promising placer deposits in the area, Barnette decided to set up a trading post along the river banks. In 1902 Pedro made a gold discovery in the Tanana Valley, 17 miles from present-day Fairbanks. Word of the discovery spread, and by the next year there was another boom camp.

The new camp was named for Charles Fairbanks of Indiana, then Vice President of the United States. Judge James Wickersham moved the U.S. Court from Eagle to Fairbanks, an act that allowed the new camp to continue to exist when many other camps died.

Winter snow trails from Eagle, Circle, Valdez, and other regions were beaten down. With the coming of spring, riverboats from St. Michael and Dawson carried the stampeders, and Fairbanks became a trading center.

Later, as delegate to the U.S. Congress from Alaska, Judge Wickersham was active in promoting the construction of the 470-mile railroad from Seward to Fairbanks to "open up the Interior." Begun in 1914, the railroad was completed in 1923, making possible the transportation of huge machinery, such as dredges, to rework the creeks that had been scratched by primitive mining methods.

Because Fairbanks is the center of interior air and road routes, regular and charter air trips depart from it to many outlying villages. Among the excursions are flights to the Indian villages of Minto and Tanana, Chena Hot Springs, Circle Hot Springs, Eagle, and the Arctic; rail, bus, and car rides to Nenana; and air, rail, or auto tours to Denali National Park and Preserve.

Arrangements for hunting, canoeing, and fishing trips can be made through private charters.

Where to stay

Several dozen hotels, including some modern newcomers, and a few motels offer many rooms. But you'll need reservations during the summer. Rates are high, even for Alaska.

Many hotels include restaurants and lounges, and independent eating places and clubs are scattered throughout the city. Again, the price is higher than you might expect.

About a dozen public and private campgrounds in Fairbanks are available for overnight use. Some offer hookups.

You'll find all the services you may need—dry cleaners, laundromats, supermarkets, and department stores. You'll also pay more for goods here than anywhere in Alaska, except the Arctic.

What's in town?

At the visitor information center, First and Cushman streets, you'll find free brochures, maps, and tips on what to see and how to get there. The city has a good bus system.

Passengers disembark *from Discovery sternwheeler trip taken near Fairbanks.*

Segment *of Alaska pipeline is highlight of Fairbanks city tour.*

The city is so spread out that you'll need a car for exploring unless you're with a tour group. Even if you're on your own, you'll find it informative to take a comprehensive tour and revisit points that interest you at a later date.

Typical bus tours of Fairbanks last about 2½ hours. Tours include downtown attractions, residential areas, a visit to the pipeline, and a stop at the museum on the University of Alaska campus. You can make arrangements in advance on prepackaged tours or buy tickets at your hotel.

The attractive University of Alaska is really worth more time than you get on a sightseeing excursion. In the museum (free admission) you'll discover one of the state's best collections of pioneer relics and of Eskimo, Aleut, and Indian artifacts. Look, too, for notable displays of northern wildlife. History buffs will want to visit the collection of many rare, old books on Alaska's beginnings in the Elmer Rasmuson Library.

Also near the campus is the Experimental Station of the U.S. Department of Agriculture. Here

research continues on developing crop strains especially suited to northern soils and climates.

At Alaskaland, on the banks of the Chena River, you can visit a log cabin town created from relocated log cabins built during Gold Rush days. Other attractions include a replica of an Eskimo village; the old sternwheeler *Nenana*, one-time queen of the Yukon River fleet, now housing a restaurant and lounge; "Mining Valley" gold rush town, where gold-mining equipment is on display and visitors can pan their own gold; collections of ancient and modern Alaskan art and artifacts; and various exhibit halls and theaters. Alaskaland covers about 40 acres, encircled by its own railroad—the Crooked Creek & Whiskey Island Line. Admission is free.

Several years ago a domed building was erected as the home for the Eskimo Olympics, held during Golden Days celebration in July. To compete for awards a contestant must be at least one-quarter native. The only exception is the muktuk (whale blubber) eating contest—which is open to anyone with a hearty appetite.

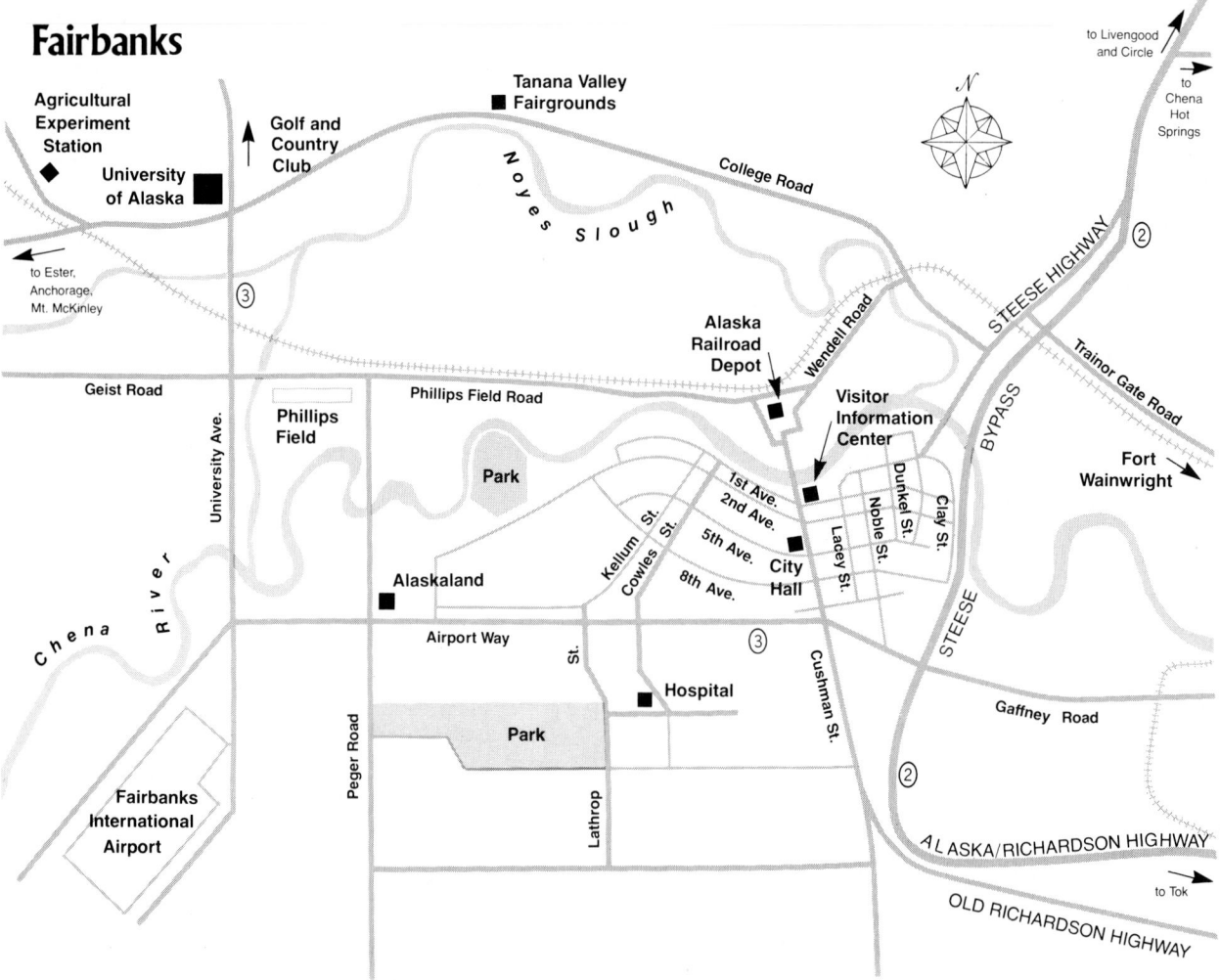

View the midnight sun

You can travel 162 miles from Fairbanks to Circle City over the partially paved Steese Highway. Sixteen miles out is Pedro Monument, rising at the site of the first gold discovery in Tanana Valley.

This road crosses Cleary and Eagle summits. In mid-June, when the weather is clear, you can see the midnight sun from Eagle Summit (elevation 3,880 feet). During the summer solstice (June 20 to 22), when the sun is at its greatest distance north of the celestial equator, the sun slowly circles the northern horizon.

The sky takes on a twilight glow as the sun dips down to the west; but instead of setting, the sun swings laterally along the horizon to a due north position at midnight, never once lost to view. The long sunset then becomes sunrise, the orb moves on to the eastern sky, and a new day begins.

From the barren crest of Eagle Summit, you have an unobstructed view across the low-lying valley of the Yukon River to the northern horizon. In the fall, migrating caribou cross the summit.

The road drops down into the Yukon watershed. From Mile 109 the roadway to the small town of Central has been widened, passing by historic Miller House, founded in 1896. Here an active mining district thrived in early days. Thirteen miles beyond Miller House is Central, a small, old-time settlement. From here a branch road leads to Circle Hot Springs.

Circle Hot Springs, discovered in 1893 by a prospector trailing a wounded moose, soon became a popular winter and summer resort.

Its mineral waters still attract visitors. Hot water piped under a large garden plot gives vegetables an early start in spring so they grow to tremendous size during the short summer.

Arctic Circle Hot Springs Resort offers a lodge with indoor swimming pool, gold panning, fishing, and mineral springs.

A dining room and cocktail lounge plus large lobby are on the ground level. Outside, a camper parking area, store, garage, and airstrip complete the complex.

Circle, the end of the highway, is the northernmost point in Alaska to which it is

possible to drive from an interconnecting highway system. At Circle, you are only 50 miles south of the Arctic Circle. It has limited accommodations, a trading post, gas station, cafe, and bar.

There are several campgrounds and trail systems along the highway between Fairbanks and Circle City.

Roads to two other springs take off from the Steese Highway—Chena Hot Springs and Manley Hot Springs.

Chena Hot Springs takes its name from the nearby Chena River. The resort includes a restaurant, lounge, pool, and camping spaces. Check at the Fairbanks Chamber of Commerce for hours the resort is open— the drive is more than 60 miles.

To reach Manley Hot Springs, take the Steese Highway, turn onto the Elliott Highway (often called "the road to Nome"), and follow the road that branches off at Livengood. The hot springs are on a hillside just before town. Water temperatures average around 136°F.

Once a busy trading community during mining days, this spa is now a quiet settlement with great civic pride. The town maintains a public campground near the bridge and keeps up spacious lawns which give the locale a park-like look.

The river brings frequent travelers; the small town also receives quite a bit of air traffic from Fairbanks, about 45 minutes flying time away.

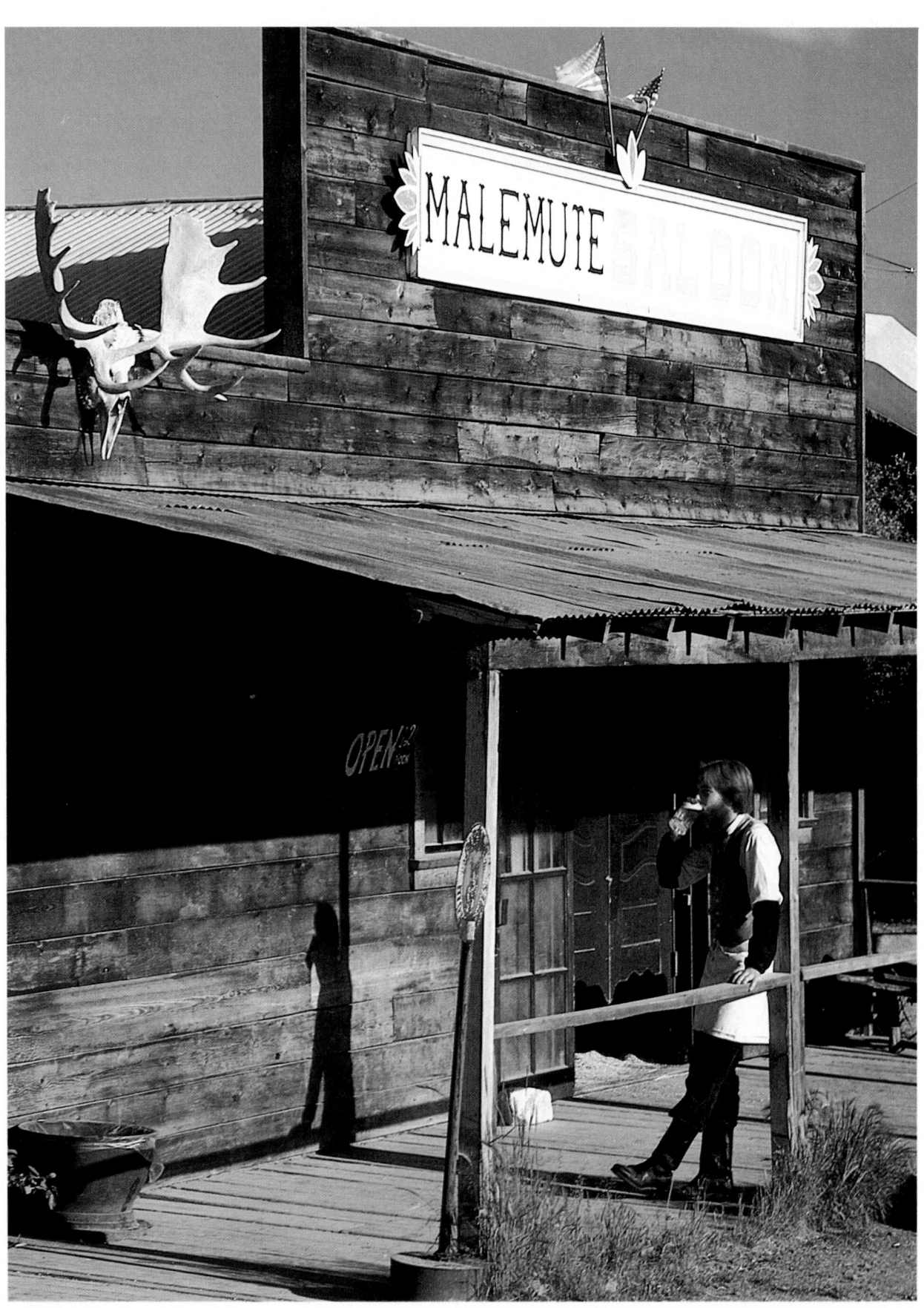

Many gift and curio shops line Fairbanks' streets. All carry a wide assortment of goods. Furriers have both raw and made-up furs and garments, including parkas, coats, jackets, stoles, hats, and other items. Local craftsmen make fine Alaskan jade and gold jewelry. Look for good ivory, too. *Qiviut*, the cashmere-soft wool of the musk ox, is spun and knit into highly prized garments. They make expensive, but unusual, gifts.

Sternwheeler riverboat cruise

Long before roads were cut through the wilderness, sternwheel paddleboats plied the riverways. Today, you can recapture the excitement and adventure of this bygone era by cruising on board an authentic reproduction of an old sternwheeler.

Alaska Riverways (Box G, Fairbanks, AK 99701), a family operation, operates sternwheeled riverboats, the *Discovery* and *Discovery II*, on daily cruises during the summer.

Your sternwheeler first heads down the Chena River to the broad Tanana, then on a 30-mile round trip into the back country—a 4-hour excursion. It stops at an Indian fishing camp where you go ashore to see a fish wheel in operation, the cleaning and drying of salmon, sled dogs, and natives at work.

Sometimes moose, bear, and beaver are sighted on this unusual trip. You will see some attractive riverbank homes, fishermen, and many small boats.

Side trips

In the immediate vicinity of Fairbanks, a network of roads includes Route 2, the Elliott Highway to Livengood (69 miles). Livengood is a former ghost town come alive again as a pipeline camp. The road continues on to Manley Hot Springs. During the summer colorful poppies bloom along the road; in July, blueberries and raspberries are thick and ready for picking.

The Steese Highway, Route 6, connects Fairbanks with Circle, a small settlement 50 miles south of the Arctic Circle (see Special Feature on page 53). It is the northernmost point in the United States that can now be reached by automobile. (The pipeline haul road, if and when opened, may allow a driving experience right into the Arctic.) Along the way you'll see sites of

Bartender at old Malemute Saloon in Ester breaks for a beer before evening rush.

former mining camps, some exceptional views, and hot springs discovered by prospectors.

About 16 miles north of Fairbanks is the spot where Felix Pedro found gold in 1902; bring along a pan to try your luck. (Much of the land is privately owned; ask permission first.)

A famous old saloon

For those with a keen interest in mining, don't miss Ester, just 7 miles west of Fairbanks on the Anchorage - Fairbanks Highway (Route 3). Once the center of the Cripple Creek mining district, the town was a bustling community of 15,000 in its heyday.

Ester is probably best known now for the Malemute Saloon, as realistic an old-time Alaskan bar as you'll find. Live entertainment includes rollicking gold rush melodies and spirited recitations of poet Robert Service's tales of the north. The hotel and bunkhouse, now modernized, take guests. You can eat dinner in the "mess hall" or in the more elegant Mine Room.

Special events

In June, you can watch a midnight baseball game played without artificial lights. The Golden Days Celebration in July commemorates Fairbanks' beginning in 1902 with Felix Pedro's nearby gold discovery. Townspeople wear old-time costumes, grow beards, and sponsor a parade and contests. Also held in July are the World Eskimo Olympic Games, a display of strength and endurance.

Denali National Park

There are higher mountains in the world but probably none that rise so monumentally as Mt. McKinley—from a valley only 1,000 feet above sea level to an altitude of 20,320 feet. It is the park's main spectacle, even at 26 miles (your closest approach by car), and overshadows other attractions of wildlife and wild scenery that are themselves reason enough for a visit.

Named "Denali" (the high one) by the Indians, the mountain was given the name McKinley in 1896 by William L. Dickey, a prospector. The name of the park surrounding this mighty mountain has been changed to Denali National Park and Preserve.

The park straddles the Alaska Range south of Fairbanks. Originally created in 1917, it was enlarged in 1932 to nearly two million acres. In 1980, under the Alaska Lands Act, the boundaries were adjusted and the park and preserve now cover 5.6 million acres.

Many visitors never get a chance to view the

mountain because of frequent cloudy, rainy summer weather (caused by the mountain itself). During periods of low visibility, your only sight of its top might be from a plane. Flying between Fairbanks and Anchorage, you can see its snowy summit rising above surrounding clouds.

Getting to the park

State Highway 3, an all-weather road, follows a direct route between Fairbanks and Anchorage, skirting the edge of the park. About 120 miles from Fairbanks (or 237 miles from Anchorage), it intersects the park road. In summer the park can be reached from Paxson along the gravel-surfaced Denali Highway.

Except for a stretch along the Susitna River, the railroad follows the same route as the highway. Vistadome cars are available on Alaska Railroad's Anchorage-McKinley-Fairbanks service. You can even arrange to ship your car by rail. Trains run daily in summer. The trip takes about 7½ hours from Anchorage or 4 hours from Fairbanks.

Your train trip can be very exciting—you may have to stop while the engineer nudges a moose out of the way. Frequent stops are also made to pick up hikers or bikers anywhere along the tracks.

Alaska-Yukon Motorcoaches and Westours Motor Coaches provide bus service to the park from either Fairbanks or Anchorage. Many pre-packaged itineraries include transportation to the park and lodging.

Scheduled air service to the park is available from Fairbanks and Anchorage. You can make a charter flightseeing tour from either city or from air taxi service near the Riley Creek Visitor Information Center.

How to cope with a grizzly

In Denali National Park, you are treading on the home territory of the grizzly. Lumbering about this wild country, these large, powerful animals are unpredictable and dangerous.

They will defend their territory, themselves, and their young. Survival is their most compelling instinct.

To reduce the chances of conflict between man and bear, you should use reasonable judgment and precaution.

The grizzly should never be surprised or closely approached. When hiking, make a lot of noise and avoid dense brush. Let the bears know where you are.

Dogs are not permitted in Denali's back country. In bear country, they could be a liability. If your pet gets into a contest with a grizzly, he may run to you in fear, perhaps bringing his opponent with him.

Prevent possible encounters by keeping away from those cuddly-looking cubs. Somewhere nearby lurks about 500 pounds of mother.

Use a telephoto lens when taking a photograph of the animal; keep your distance.

Bears eat almost anything, so keep a clean campsite. Burn refuse, and wash or burn cans to destroy odors. Carry out everything you carry in.

In camp, seal food in plastic bags and cache them somewhere other than around your immediate camp area. Eliminate food odor from yourself.

Though there are always inherent dangers in the wilderness, you will probably run into no trouble if you respect its natural beauty—and pay careful respect to the ways of its inhabitants.

What to take with you

Your visit to the park will be more enjoyable and safer if you plan ahead. Weather is variable. A layered look of warm sweater or coat underneath rain gear allows flexibility. Bring sturdy walking shoes or boots.

For hiking in the park, take along a picnic lunch and snacks, insect repellent, binoculars with a spotting scope, camera with telephoto lens and extra film—and a companion.

Where to stay

The McKinley Park Station Hotel near the eastern Riley Creek highway entrance offers a unique combination of conventional hotel rooms combined with Pullman-style railroad sleeping cars in keeping with its railroad theme. The coffee shop is a couple of done-over dining cars while the bar is actually a couple of rejuvenated lounge cars.

Private accommodations along the Anchorage-Fairbanks Highway include motels, campgrounds, and youth hostels near the park entrance.

Although the park is open year-round, visitor facilities operate only from May through September.

Other lodging just outside the park's northwestern boundary includes small North Face Lodge and Camp Denali. Camp Denali is a true wilderness camp dedicated to lovers of the outdoors. It has a main lodge, dining hall, and chalet cabins. It does *not* have running water in rooms, private showers, electricity, or indoor plumbing.

At the camp you can swim, paddle a canoe, or kayak around Wonder Lake. Hiking, studying wildflowers, photography, and nature explorations are popular activities.

Additional diversions include guided walks, mountain climbing, barbecues, fishing, and berry-picking trips. From here it's easy to visit the ghost town of Kantishna or pull yourself across rushing Moose Creek in a hand cable car. Enough gold remains in these once-rich diggings to make a try with a pan worthwhile.

Lodging is limited and advance reservations are definitely required. Check with your travel agent or tour operator.

Improved campgrounds are located along the park road between the entrance and Camp Denali. If you plan to camp in the park, you must choose a campsite and then register for it at the Visitor Orientation Center in the headquarters-entrance area. Campsites at Riley Creek, Savage River, Sanctuary River, Teklanika River, Igloo Creek, and Wonder Lake are available on a first-come, first-serve basis, but still require reservations. All reservations must be made in person at the Riley Creek Visitors Center for the visit beginning that day; no advance reservations are taken. For further information, write the Supt., Denali National Park, P.O. Box 9, Denali Park, AK 99755, or call Zenith 2344.

Rejuvenated *railroad cars house some of the guests who stay at McKinley Park Station Hotel.*

Traveling through the park

You can travel through the park in two ways—by shuttle bus or on the Wildlife Scenic Tour. Only the first 14 miles of the park road—to Savage River—are open to private vehicles. You'll have to get into the interior of the park to catch your first view of the mountain; many visitors are disappointed when they realize the mountain is not visible from the McKinley Park Station Hotel.

Motorists with reservations at a campground inside the park can drive to their campsite but must leave their cars there and use the free shuttle bus for transportation.

Buses make nine stops between the entrance and Wonder Lake. Space is available for hiking and camping equipment, and you can leave or board the bus at any of the scheduled stops or at any other point by informing the driver.

Guided wildlife tours, with knowledgeable bus drivers, are offered daily in the early morning and late afternoon. Tickets are sold at the McKinley Park Station Hotel. Your fare includes a hot meal served at the Eielson Visitor Center deep in the park. Bus trips take about 8 hours.

The classic view of Mt. McKinley is from Wonder Lake, last stop by shuttle buses. On calm days the reflection in the lake doubles the grandeur of the mountain, making it difficult to grasp its true scale.

Soon after you leave the park entrance, the road climbs up out of the spruce forest into wide open country above timberline. Your first glimpse of the mountain comes when you reach the aptly named Savage River. At Stony Pass, just beyond the Toklat River, you'll have your first full view of the mountain. At rainbow-hued Polychrome Pass, mineral colors streak the mountainside.

Viewing the wildlife

The drive along the park highway is like a visit to a great natural zoo. Here, though, only you, the visitor, are encaged; the animals roam free. About 30 miles out the park road, cliffs and crags above Igloo Creek are often white-dotted with groups of Dall sheep.

In June, caribou assemble on the tundra plains just before their annual migration northward. By the end of June, herds numbering in the hundreds can be seen grazing below Eielson Visitor Center and in the vicinity of Wonder Lake.

At Sable Pass, 35 to 40 miles from the park entrance, grizzly bears are so numerous that park officials forbid you to leave the roadway. This restriction serves the double purpose of protecting visitors from bears and lessening the

chance that the bears might be driven away from the area to seek more private surroundings.

Moose are common throughout the park. You'll frequently see these ungainly creatures knee-deep in the lowland ponds bordering the highway, plunging their heads beneath the surface of the water in search of tender water grasses. Alaskan moose are *very* big—they're the world's largest deer.

Porcupines, marmots, squirrels, foxes, snowshoe hares, coyotes, and beavers add to roadside wildlife. Youngsters will especially enjoy watching beavers. In early morning and late afternoon, you'll see them busily at work in the dozens of small, tundra-bordered lakes around 70 miles from the park entrance.

Birds in great variety, including many species of nesting waterfowl, make their summer homes within the park boundaries. Year-round residents include the golden eagle, ptarmigan, and great horned owl. Unusual migrants include the Arctic warbler and European wheatear (from Asia), the golden plover (from Hawaii), and the long-tailed jaeger (from Japan).

What to do in the park

A current schedule of visitor activities is posted at the visitor center and the hotel. In addition to making the wildlife tour, a one or two-day stop allows for campfire talks, short hikes on several trails departing from the hotel, and sled dog demonstrations by rangers.

Experienced hikers and campers enjoy getting into the back country. You'll need a use permit for overnight hiking trips. Get the permit and information on current hiking conditions from the Riley Creek Visitor Orientation Center.

Camp away from the road; people traveling through the park did not come to see brightly colored tents. Whatever you carry in, you must carry out. Campfires are restricted to emergencies; carry along a small stove and fuel.

For mountaineering or glacial travel above 12,000 feet, you're required to register at park headquarters. Special equipment and knowledge are necessary for traversing glaciers and snow fields.

Fishing is not good in most park rivers because of the milky, pulverized silt they usually carry. Arctic grayling can be caught in a few clear mountain streams, and trout are taken from Wonder Lake. You don't need a license.

No hunting is permitted in park boundaries. Don't bring in firearms.

Hills of Fire tour, a 2½-hour narrated bus excursion departs from McKinley Park Station Hotel, Mt. McKinley Village (outside the park), or other

(Continued on page 63)

Solitary moose, *usually found among trees and brush, wanders through soggy tundra.*

Blonde Toklat grizzly *sow stands up to survey terrain for possible danger to her cubs.*

The controversial pipeline

Although 800 miles of 48-inch pipe may seem inconsequential in a state as vast as Alaska, the impact of the Alaska pipeline on Alaskan economic and social conditions has been enormous.

Almost bisecting the state, the controversial pipeline winds from the Arctic region of Prudhoe Bay to the ice-free port of Valdez. In Valdez the oil is stored to await passage on tankers to various ports in California and the state of Washington.

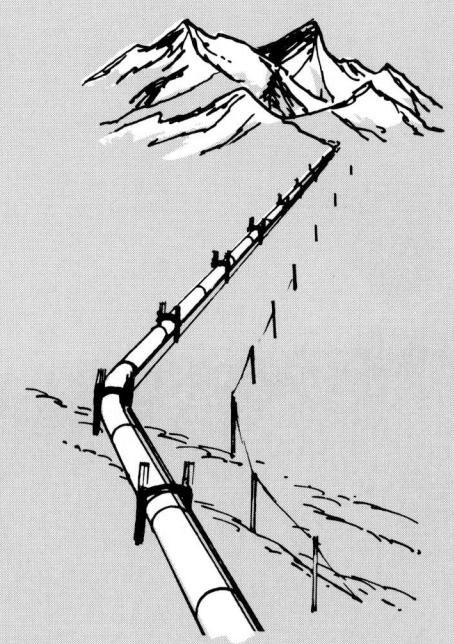

A new gold rush

One Alaskan has declared that "pipeline construction is the most important economic phenomenon to happen to Alaska since the Gold Rush." A contemporary "Eureka" was first shouted in the summer of 1968, when two major oil companies—Atlantic Richfield and British Petroleum—struck oil 8,000 to 10,000 feet below the tundra at Prudhoe Bay.

Declaring it the greatest oil strike ever made in North America, experts speculated that 9.7 billion barrels of recoverable oil and 25.4 trillion cubic feet of natural gas lay beneath the surface. Oil companies soon envisioned a pipeline carrying 1.2 million barrels a day to help quench the national thirst.

Oil and natural gas make up about three-quarters of the United State's energy needs. Experts believe that the current daily crude oil consumption of 17 million barrels a day will rise to about 24 million. Although Prudhoe Bay oil will not make the nation independent of foreign oil imports, it will be a major addition to domestic oil production.

Construction of a pipeline

After major oil companies formed the Alyeska Pipeline Service Company to build and operate the pipeline, hundreds of men and women were hired to create one of the most technologically sophisticated undertakings of this kind in history.

The pipeline is built to withstand the often cruel Alaskan climate, in which temperatures can range from 90°F. to minus 60°F. For almost half of its 800 miles, the pipeline travels above ground on thousands of vertical supports planted in sensitive permafrost. Friction generated by pumping pressure keeps the oil at about 140°F.; in addition, the pipe is heavily insulated to maintain a pumpable temperature in case of stoppage.

But before any of this construction could proceed, certain legal and political problems needed to be solved. One fundamental question was, "Who owns Alaska?" Native organizations claimed that neither the Alaska Purchase nor the Statehood Act established the land rights of natives living for generations in Alaska. Until ownership could be determined, Secretary of the Interior Stuart Udall halted all transfers of land and leases. This decision united the strangest bedfellows in Alaskan history—the major oil companies and native Alaskans.

Realizing the potential cost of any construction delay, the major oil companies resolutely lobbied on behalf of the natives. The result was the Native Claims Settlement Act of 1971. This act created 13 native-owned, profit-making corporations, endowed with one billion dollars in revenue and 40 million acres of land.

Although the natives and the Alaskan government welcomed this cash inflow as a solution to many economic and social needs, environmentalists remained unappeased, fearing that the pipeline would threaten the very fragile ecosystem of Alaska.

Environmental challenges

For four years, construction of the pipeline was blocked by a flurry of suits against Alyeska, as environmentalists challenged the integrity of the company's plan. They pointed out that the flowing temperature of oil— about 140°F.— could easily thaw permafrost, endangering the structural stability of the line. Then, too, the pipeline would run through the Denali Fault, a region of potentially high earthquake activity, where in the past earthquakes have struck within 50 miles of the pipeline route. A major break could spill as much as 90,000 barrels of oil over Alaskan terrain.

Because the pipeline would also run through the Brooks Range, one of the United State's few remaining stretches of wilderness, environmentalists felt it might disrupt the migration of large caribou and other animals. And since the oil was to travel in tankers from Valdez, the threat of oil spills at sea was ever-present.

Despite these fears, investment in the pipeline was substantial enough that construction seemed inevitable. In November, 1973, Congress, pressured by diminished domestic production along with increased consumption of oil and, more importantly, the Arab oil embargo with the resulting price increase, passed the Pipeline Authorization Act.

A company's concerns

Though the oil companies were not legally required to do so, they made extensive revisions of design to respond to conservationists' concerns. Alyeska changed its original plan of running 95 percent of the pipe underground to running 50 percent above ground, lessening the danger that the oil might thaw the permafrost. The company claims the pipeline can withstand earthquake shocks registering 8.5 on the Richter scale, but —if a break should occur—hundreds of automatic valves would cut off the oil.

In addition, Alyeska took measures to anchor the tanker terminal at Valdez in bedrock and to surround the storage tanks with large dikes to contain spills, should they occur.

As the pipeline neared completion in the spring of 1976, yet another controversy reared up. News leaked out that, in the rush to complete construction, critically important sections of pipe were welded improperly. After a congressional investigation and a construction delay, Alyeska replaced or repaired 30 percent of the pipeline's welds.

These precautionary measures, along with inflated paychecks and other costly delays, ballooned the estimated pipeline cost of 1.5 billion dollars to an actual cost of 9 billion dollars.

Oil's effect on the state

Oil first flowed through the pipeline in late June, 1977. During the first days of operation, an explosion occurred, resulting in a fire and minimal damage that was soon repaired. Since this initial incident, the pipeline has operated smoothly.

With the discovery of oil, the "get rich quick" mania has again invaded Alaska. Economists claim that the pipeline project has propelled Alaska towards a higher economic plane. Estimates are that soon government spending will increase ten-fold over that of 1970.

But development is not only measured in dollars and cents. Like all booms, the oil boom in Alaska is accompanied by social change. One side effect of the newly acquired wealth is an inflation rate higher than that of any state in the Lower 48. Alaska has also seen dramatic increases in population, housing shortages, alcoholism, and crime.

Visitors *inspect Alyeska pipeline a short distance out of Fairbanks. Where it is buried in the background, pipeline is refrigerated to keep hot oil from thawing permafrost.*

Tired of pedaling, *bikers hitch ride on Alaska Railroad. Train runs between Fairbanks and Seward, stops for passengers in town or whenever hailed along the tracks.*

Broad highway *between Fairbanks and Anchorage appears to end abruptly at towering Alaska Range.*

...Continued from page 58

surrounding facilities and campsites; taking you to the Usibelli Coal Mine at nearby Healy.

A successful reclamation project, begun in 1971, has drawn nearly 100 Dall sheep to graze on grassy hillsides where only a few years ago there was raw evidence of strip mining. The bus passes vein-streaked hills where the coal occasionally bursts into spontaneous flame, giving this area its name.

Visitors can watch giant earthmoving machinery in action in this model mine for the future. You'll also get enticing glimpses of alpine meadows and mountain streams. At the tour's conclusion you may want to sample an unusual treat—coal candy.

Air flights over Mt. McKinley give you an ever greater appreciation for the mountain. Denali Flying Service, operating from an airstrip near the McKinley Park railroad station, offers two basic sightseeing tours. The Muldrow Glacier flight (about 1 hour) gives an eagle's eye view of the north side of Mt. McKinley. The Ruth Amphitheater flight (approximately 1¾ hours) completely circles the mountain. Early in the morning (weather permitting) the best flight and photographic conditions prevail.

The Anchorage–Fairbanks Highway

The George Parks Highway is the official name of Alaska Route 3. However, because the highway connects Alaska's two largest cities, it has been better known as the Anchorage - Fairbanks Highway since its completion in 1971.

This scenic roadway runs through 358 miles of some of the grandest and most rugged land Alaska has to offer. It passes through the Talkeetna Mountains and the Alaska Range, over many rushing streams, and alongside meadows filled with wildflowers in the spring. Rewarding sights range from elegant stands of white birches to glimpses of the great glaciers that feed the rivers. Mt. McKinley becomes visible to motorists heading north when they are about an hour away from Anchorage.

The highway is well engineered and maintained for year-round driving. Even so, winter motorists should check road conditions by calling the Alaska State Highway Department in Anchorage or Fairbanks. In summertime, the road is usually under repair at some point due to "frost heaves."

The Alaska Railroad and the highway intersect again and again on their paths between the two cities. Both follow along the courses of some major rivers.

From Anchorage to Fairbanks

After passing through the fertile Matanuska Valley you reach the pioneer town of Wasilla, heralded as the fastest-growing town in the nation. From a hamlet with less than a thousand people a little over a year ago, Wasilla has mushroomed into a city complete with its own fly-in, drive-in shopping mall.

Bordered on two sides by blue fishing lakes, the country around Wasilla is polka-dotted with cabins, trailers, and houses. It has almost become a suburb of Anchorage.

For a taste of real Alaskana, stop by Teeland's Country Store. Serving miners, railroaders, and homesteaders since 1905, it is now modernized and filled with original photographs, antiques, and artifacts.

From Wasilla, the highway enters the Talkeetna Mountains. Hatcher Pass Road (also called Willow Road East) circles between Willow and Wasilla through gold mining country. Though the mines are closed, "color" can still be found.

Willow was the site selected as the state's new capital; you'll see much new construction and a number of real estate signs along the highway.

After mining slacked off in the early 1940s, Willow became a virtual ghost town until the completion of the highway. You'll find a couple of spots in town for cocktails, food, and dancing. Willow sponsors an annual winter carnival that features dog mushing, cross country skiing, wood chopping contests, and other festivities.

About 30 miles from Willow, the Talkeetna Spur Road leads to the town of Talkeetna, noted for its crooked streets, log buildings, and early-day pioneer atmosphere. Another side road farther on ends at the old mining camp of Petersville.

Talkeetna residents fight to preserve the flavor of the town, which is now a historical site—but with the proposed new state capital situated nearby it may be a losing battle.

Many McKinley climbing expeditions start here. Ski-wheel aircraft depart from Talkeetna for Kahlitna Glacier, depositing passengers and gear for the climb up the West Buttress Route to the summit of South Peak. You can find a guide in Talkeetna, but before you make the climb you must contact the Superintendent of Denali National Park (P.O. Box 9, Denali Park, AK 99755) for permission.

Denali State Park, scene of past and present glacial activity, is bisected by the Parks Highway. Though the park is a game refuge, few large animals are seen from the highway. Moose retreat to higher elevations, caribou have migrated

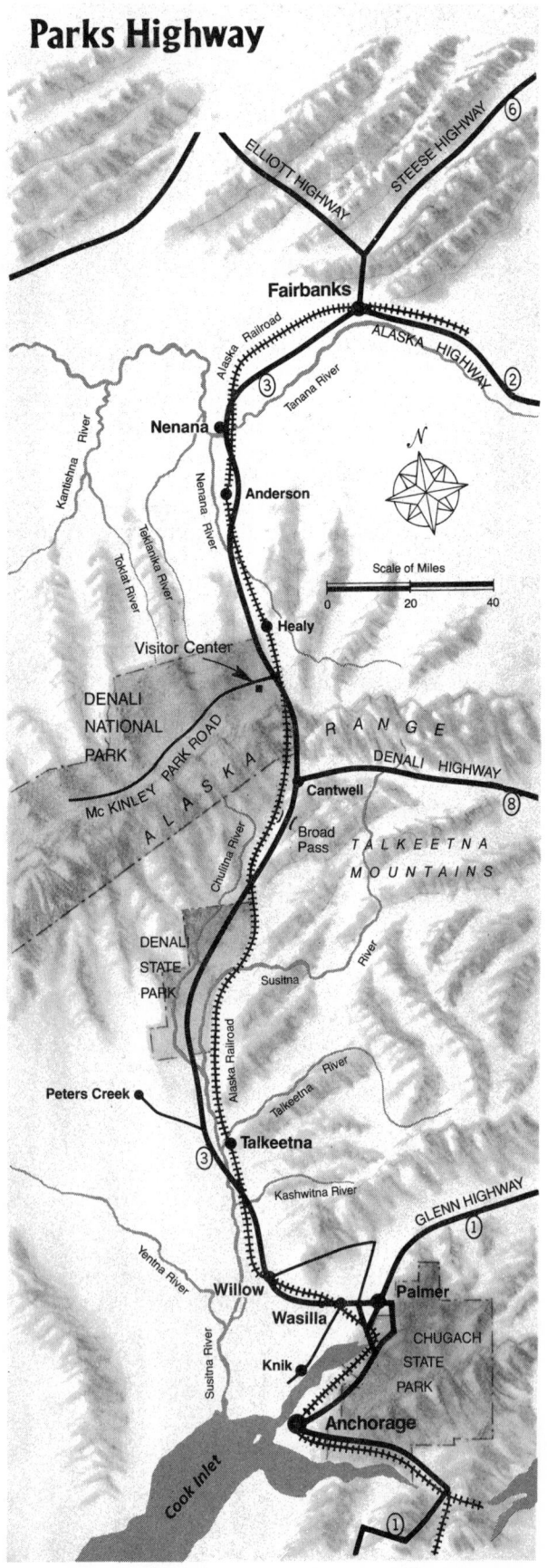

Parks Highway

north, wolves hide from civilization, and bear prefer a more remote habitat.

Though the park is relatively undeveloped, there is a state campground at Byers Lake. In summer the bearded spruce, huge cottonwood, and lush undergrowth give the area the appearance of a tropical rain forest. Campsites, nestled into the forest, are new, equipped with fireplaces and outdoor toilets. A trail leads up to a butte above the lake, giving a good view of great Mt. McKinley.

Only one lodge is now located in this wilderness, although plans are in the works for a future hotel. The name of the lodge—McKinley View—spells out its setting.

Once through 2,343-foot Broad Pass you reach the turnoff to McKinley Park Highway. Both the highway and railroad follow this pass through the Alaska Range.

For several miles the road crosses and recrosses the Nenana River. At the far side of the second bridge (northbound from Anchorage), is the boundary of Denali National Park. For almost 7 miles from this point the highway is within the park boundaries. No discharge of firearms is permitted. Many parking areas are provided for rest stops and mountain-viewing.

When you are about 10 miles along the way to Fairbanks, watch out for strong winds over the Moody Bridge-Nenana Bridge Number 4. State Highway 3 passes Healy, in the center of the coal mining area. Nearby, you can take the Hills of Fire tour to the Usibelli Coal Mine for a look at burning hills, flowering meadows, and alpine streams.

Nenana—site of the breakup

About 60 miles farther along you enter Nenana. This old river port came into being in 1916 on the site of an Indian village. It was the construction base for the northern part of the Alaska Railroad, completed in 1923. During open-water season, river freight traffic is still important to the little town.

Stop at the visitor center for coffee and information on the "Big Breakup" ceremony each spring when the thaw sets in on the Tanana River.

Nenana's gigantic Ice Pool (legal for residents of Alaska only) is the largest in the world, usually offering $100,000 in cash prizes to lucky winners who can guess the exact minute of the ice breakup.

On an unpredictable day in April or May the surging ice dislodges a tripod set in the river, and an attached line stops a clock, marking the official time of breakup.

Although the icy guessing game is Nenana's

chief claim to fame, the town boasts other assets as well. Geography places it at the head of one of Alaska's most scenic valleys, dominated by miles-high Mt. McKinley on the southwestern horizon. Sportsmen find good hunting in the game-rich valley where moose, caribou, Dall sheep, black bear, and Toklat grizzlies abound.

Visitors can watch fish wheels scooping up salmon from the currents of the Tanana River. Fresh and smoked salmon are for sale during late summer and early fall.

Back on the highway, you'll be headed for Fairbanks, only 60 miles away. Because of the flat land, you'll get vivid city views long before you reach the town.

Curiosity *works both ways. Twin fox kits in Denali National Park may never have seen man before.*

Typical roadside stop *between Anchorage and Fairbanks attracts souvenir shoppers. Fishwheel in foreground is Indian device for scooping up salmon. "Cache" on stilts in rear protects food from animals.*

In & around Anchorage

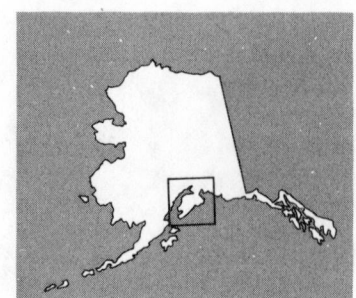

Anchorage, Alaska's largest city, is often a visitor's introduction to the state. A modern metropolis, Anchorage surprises the first-time tourist. With its large airport, multilaned freeways, and skyscrapers, it reminds people of cities in the "Lower 48."

There is no long history here; most of its 200,000 residents are progressive newcomers, presenting a cross-section of life in the 49th state.

The city's location is dramatic. Situated on a benchland 30 feet above high tide, Cook Inlet acts as its front door and the Chugach Range forms a backdrop. Anchorage commands a view of the Talkeetna Mountains and the snow-capped Alaska Range to the north.

Two muddy branches of the inlet (Knik and Turnagain arms) surround the broad peninsula on which the city lies. Southeast, both the paved Seward Highway and the Alaska Railroad skirt the north shore of Turnagain Arm (aptly named by Captain Cook who discovered it while seeking a Northwest Passage).

It's 48 miles to Portage where the highway and railroad swing south onto the Kenai Peninsula. To the east, the Kenai Mountains conceal the fact that this peninsula is connected to the Alaskan mainland by a strip of land barely 10 miles wide.

Severely damaged by the 1964 Good Friday earthquake, Anchorage and the gulf area bounced back remarkably. Today, quake damage is almost impossible to find. Cities and roads were rebuilt or relocated.

Highways to the interior start in Anchorage. You follow the Anchorage-Fairbanks Highway to reach Mt. McKinley National Park. The Glenn Highway stretches eastward to meet the scenic Richardson Highway leading to Valdez. (A land-water combination excursion on the Glenn, Richardson, and Seward highways makes an enjoyable two-day circle.)

Anchorage is Alaska's metropolis

Dubbed "Air Crossroads of the World," Anchorage acts as a jumping-off spot to other parts of the state. From here it's easy to reach Southeast Alaska, the Arctic, the Kenai Peninsula, Alaska Peninsula, Kodiak Island, and the Aleutian and Pribilof islands. Mt. McKinley and Fairbanks are only a short distance by air.

International airlines make stopovers at the Anchorage airport; scheduled interstate air carriers reach the "Lower 48"; and a half-dozen intra-Alaska airlines as well as many bush pilots headquarter there.

Anchorage is a center for the Alaska Railroad. Trains run daily in the summer from Anchorage to Denali National Park and Fairbanks to the north, and from Anchorage to Whittier on Turnagain Arm.

Sleep, eat, and dance

You'll find plenty of places to stay—many quite plush. The Anchorage Westward Hilton, Captain Cook, and the new Sheraton all qualify as luxury hotels. Be sure you have hotel reservations during summer or during the annual Fur Rendezvous in February.

Camping is easy. Several public and private campgrounds and camper parks are in or near the city—and wilderness lies only minutes away. At Chugach State Park, east of Anchorage, you

Dusk outlines *Anchorage skyline and Chugach mountain backdrop. Alaska's largest city faces Cook Inlet.*

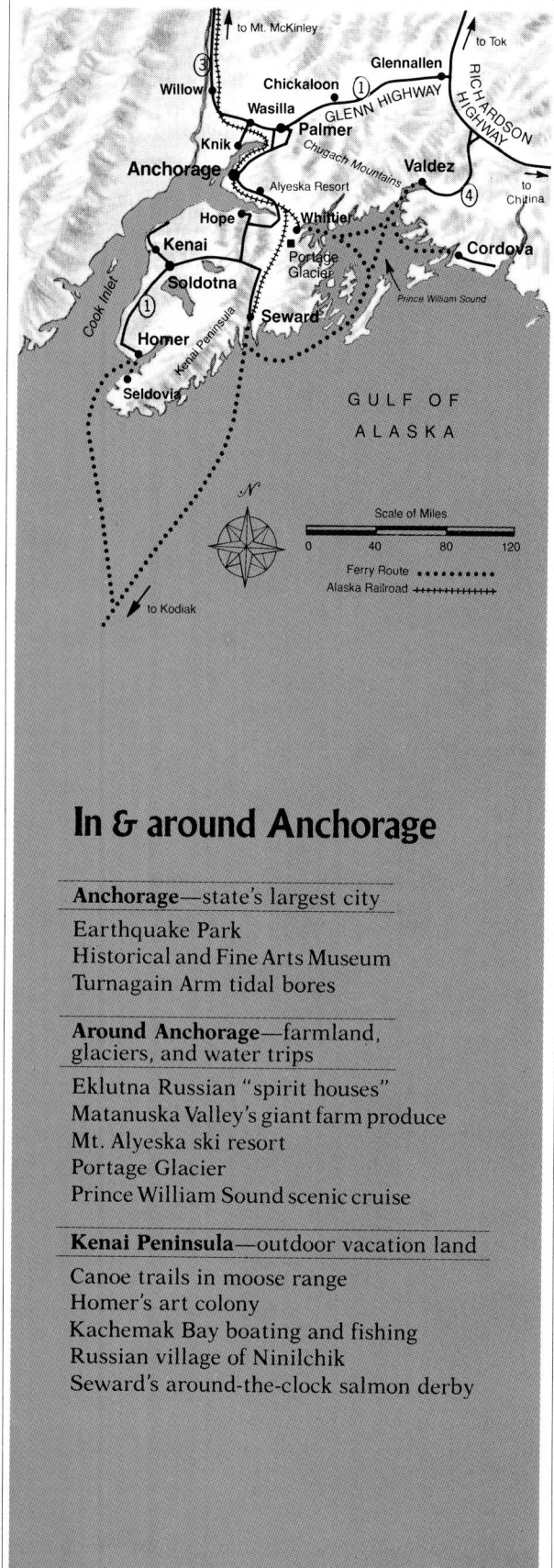

In & around Anchorage

Anchorage—state's largest city

Earthquake Park
Historical and Fine Arts Museum
Turnagain Arm tidal bores

Around Anchorage—farmland,
glaciers, and water trips

Eklutna Russian "spirit houses"
Matanuska Valley's giant farm produce
Mt. Alyeska ski resort
Portage Glacier
Prince William Sound scenic cruise

Kenai Peninsula—outdoor vacation land

Canoe trails in moose range
Homer's art colony
Kachemak Bay boating and fishing
Russian village of Ninilchik
Seward's around-the-clock salmon derby

can watch wildlife, pick blueberries, hike, fish, ski, dog sled, or go snowmobiling, depending upon the season. Established campgrounds in the park are at Eklutna River, Eagle River, and Bird Creek. You'll also find over 30 Forest Service cabins in the Chugach National Forest (see page 25).

Dining is a delight. In addition to hotel dining rooms and several good seafood restaurants, Anchorage offers a variety of continental cuisine. (Be prepared for some of Alaska's high prices.) You'll also discover your favorite hamburger, pizza, or fried chicken chain.

Alaska's nightlife is best in this city. The major hotels feature shows and dancing (live Alaska Story at the Captain Cook needs reservations). Music ranges from rock to Western to pops. Most night clubs offer entertainment. The range of drinking establishments offers something for everyone. It's best to avoid 4th Avenue's dreary saloons.

Around town

Anchorage is a city of contrasts and contradictions. Fancy hotels and rooftop restaurants overlook salmon-spawning streams. Swarms of wild birds nest in lakes that boast an awesome collection of noisy floatplanes.

Anchorage's compact, neatly laid out downtown makes it surprisingly easy to find your way around. Maps are readily available at the airport, car rental agencies, service stations, hotels, or the Anchorage Convention & Visitors Bureau Information Center (a sod-roofed log cabin at 4th Avenue and F Street). Call (907) 276-3200 for a recorded message suggesting attractions.

Take a tour. Gray Line of Anchorage offers two-hour city tours covering downtown and surrounding residential areas. You'll see views of Cook Inlet, earthquake damage, Turnagain Arm, the university, and Lakes Spenard and Hood (home of the floatplanes).

See Earthquake Park. At the west end of Northern Lights Boulevard, you'll find the 132-acre Earthquake Park (on Knik Arm), a good place to see what happened during the 1964 earthquake. On a clear day it's also a good place to catch a view of Mt. McKinley. You stroll through the park on gravel walkways among mounds of earth covered with slanted trees and brush—grim reminders of nature's force.

See the wildlife. Anchorage's zoo contains over 35 species of wildlife (some not native to Alaska) on five wooded acres. Located on O'Malley Road, 2 miles off the Seward Highway, the zoo is open daily, except Tuesday, from 11 a.m. to 5 p.m.

Elmendorf Air Force Base Wildlife Museum, open weekdays, displays native Alaskan species from big game to small birds. Fort Richardson Army Post Wildlife Museum allows photos of all displayed animals. It's open Tuesday through Saturday from noon to 7 p.m.

Pick a park. At Russian Jack Springs you can golf on a 9-hole course with artificial turf greens. This becomes a cross-country ski course in winter. An amazing variety of tropical plants, fish, and birds thrives here in the city's greenhouse.

Check the Yellow Pages for bicycle rentals and try one of the winding bike paths through Russian Jack Springs, on the Campbell Creek Greenbelt, or along the Chester Creek Greenbelt in Mulcahy Park.

Visit a museum. The Historical and Fine Arts Museum, 121 W. 7th Ave., houses many rare artifacts and selected native arts and crafts. Open 12 hours daily during summer, this rich cultural repository is a "must see."

Art and artifacts are also on display during the week at the Heritage Library of the National Bank of Alaska (5th Avenue and E Street).

Alaska Arctic Indian & Eskimo Museum, 819 W. 4th Ave., contains Arctic wildlife mounts and Eskimo artifacts; a gift shop and ivory workshop adjoins.

Watch a tidal bore. One of nature's best shows, Turnagain Arm's tidal range approaches 40 feet. Timing is all-important to catch the changing tide; check the local newspaper for low tide. Though the rising tide rushing in over the mud flats in a formidable wall of water makes interesting viewing, it's hazardous for boaters. Don't plan to walk around on the mud flats; you might suddenly be in over your head.

Sample the shops. Numerous gift stores around town contain much of the best in Alaskan arts and crafts, along with some of the worst in tourist trinkets. Buying pieces with the "Silver Hand" tag assures authentic native craftsmanship.

You'll find ivory and soapstone carvings, fur,

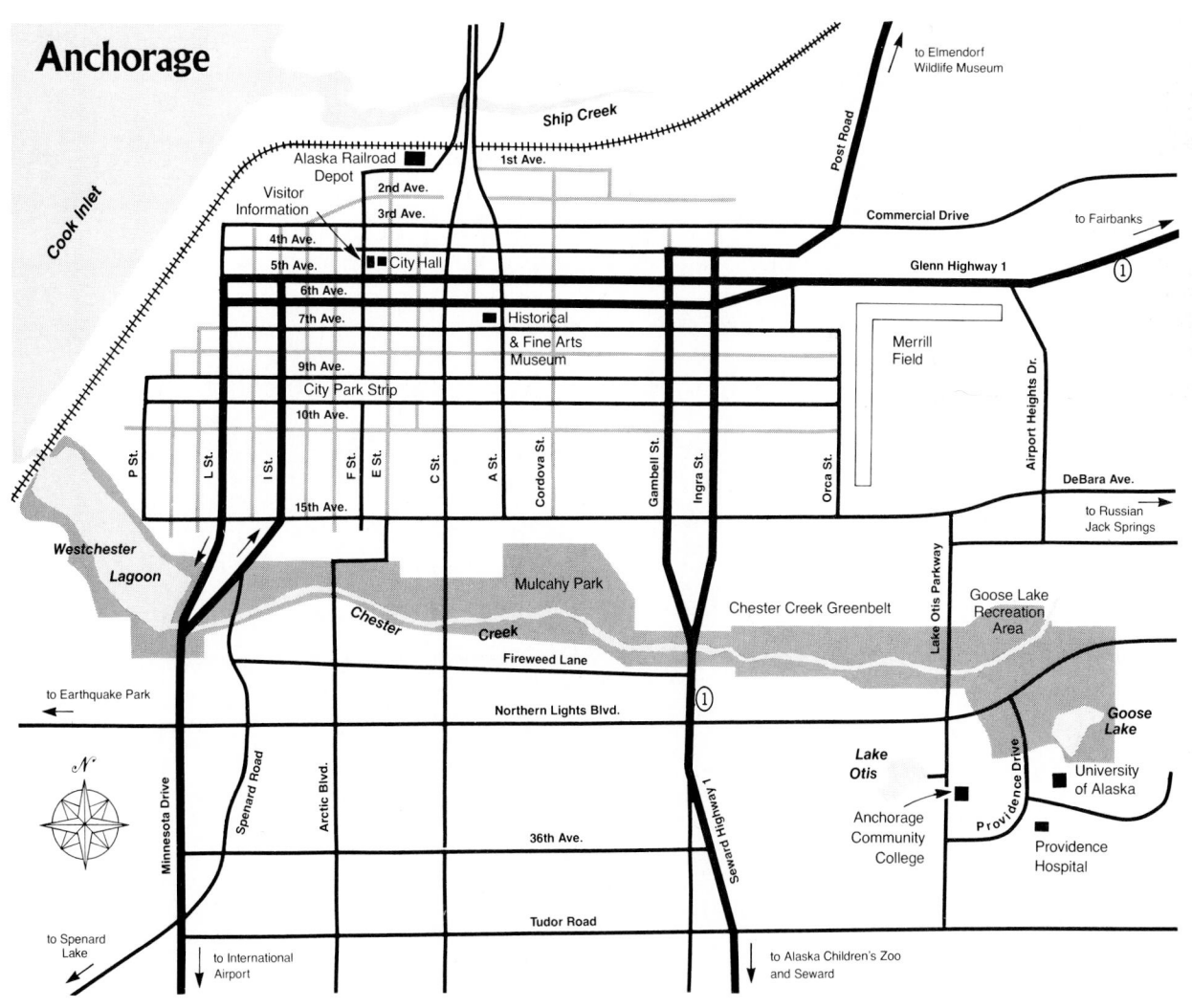

Rare pastoral scene *is Matanuska
Valley, noted for giant vegetables.*

Colorful flowers *in downtown
Anchorage thrive in long daylight
hours of summer.*

gold nugget and jade jewelry, paintings, parkas, and pottery. Interesting shops include The Gilded Cage (Eskimo dancers perform daily, except Sunday, at noon), Wright Alaskan Parky, Anchorage Fur Factory (free tour and souvenir), Artique, Ltd., The Eskimo Shop, and Alaska Native Arts and Crafts (native craft outlet).

Two very special events

A couple of festivals, one in winter, another in summer, show two contrasting sides of Alaska: the frontier and the cultural.

Fur Rendezvous, an annual February event, celebrates the fact that Anchorage is a gathering point for buyers from the world's fashion centers who come to bid on the wealth of furs produced in the 49th state. Public auctions take place on the steps of City Hall.

Musical chants of Eskimos mingle with yapping of harnessed dog teams. The World Champion Sled Dog Races held during "Rondy" attract "mushers" from all over the state. Alaska's largest winter celebration also has a snowshoe baseball game, Miners and Trappers Ball, art show, wrestling, Eskimo dances, and blanket toss exhibitions. (See Special Feature on page 45.) For festival dates, write to Fur Rendezvous, Box 773, Anchorage, AK 99510.

The Alaska Festival of Music, held in June of each year, features two weeks of concerts, recitals, theater, jazz, dance, opera, film, and visual arts. Outstanding artists include performers from Asia and Europe. For information, write to Alaska Festival of Music, 608 W. 4th Ave., Anchorage, AK 99501.

Excursions from Anchorage

Boat to the face of a sparkling blue glacier; have lunch at one of Alaska's few farms; visit the state's largest ski resort; photograph an iceberg lake. All these adventures wait for you just a few hours outside of Anchorage.

Using the city as a base, you can easily make one or two-day trips into the surrounding countryside. Complete package itineraries to Matanuska Valley, Portage Glacier, Mt. Alyeska, and Prince William Sound are offered by Gray Line of Anchorage. These include transportation, lodging, and sightseeing.

Vacations in the back country

Using Anchorage as a base, the visitor to central Alaska can be quite choosy about his back country excursions. Charter air services in Anchorage will take parties to remote lakes or rivers for fishing, rafting, swimming, or sightseeing.

Water excursions. Travelers can join organized raft trips on rivers such as the Chulitna, Little Susitna, or Kenai. These wilderness excursions generally include guides, meals, waterproof pack for gear, and transportation to and from Anchorage.

Plan to spend around 3 days on an organized voyage; you can take a 1-day kayak or raft trip on the Portage River.

Some air charters in Anchorage will take your group to a lake or river for an unguided float trip. They drop you off with raft and supplies, retrieving you a few days later at a designated point.

Pick your own spot; most air charters will take you anywhere they can land a floatplane. Ask the pilots for favorite fishing or floating spots. You'll probably find a place in the wilderness where you won't run into another person.

Backpacking trips. From Anchorage, several guide services specialize in hiking, mountain climbing, and backpacking. Your possible adventures include a 1-day trip into the wilderness just outside Anchorage, a 12-day mountain climb, or an 8-day hike across the Harding Icefield.

Trips generally include transportation to and from Anchorage, food, shelter, and gear. For additional information on experienced back country guides, check with the Anchorage Chamber of Commerce.

Off-season excursions. Many visitors are discovering the adventure of off-season travel. Fall brings brilliant colors, hunting, and good fishing. Most tours stop operating, but accommodations are much easier to find.

Winter months are dark and cold. To compensate, Alaskans amuse themselves with festivals and outdoor sporting events. Visitors are welcomed as a contact with the outside world.

Again, Anchorage is a good base of operations for early and late season travel. Mt. Alyeska, Alaska's largest ski resort, is only 40 miles away. Other downhill and cross-country skiing is as close as 10 minutes from your hotel. The parkways winding through town make excellent cross-country ski trails.

Ice-fishing in the countless lakes around town is another popular winter sport. You'll need an ice chisel, rod, line, bait, hooks, and warm clothing—plus a fishing license.

Tour a gold mine

You can take a package sightseeing excursion from Anchorage to the Independence Mine, last region in Alaska to be developed for hard rock gold mining.

The 6-hour trip departs from downtown Anchorage hotels daily during the summer season.

It includes a motor coach journey into the Talkeetna Mountains with a stop for lunch at a scenic viewpoint. You receive a 2-hour guided tour of the mine which has been dormant for over 30 years. Twenty miles of tunnels and a number of large buildings still stand.

Into the Matanuska Valley

Alaska's largest farming region lies some 40 miles northeast of Anchorage. Nestled amidst rugged, glacially carved peaks, this lush valley was primarily settled in the 1930s by drought-stricken Midwest farmers.

Though the growing season lasts only four months, long daylight hours produce record-size vegetables—turnips more than 7 pounds, cabbages 70 pounds, and huge potatoes.

Palmer is the trading center for this agricultural community. Early each fall the city plays host to the Alaska State Fair. On display are over 5,000 agricultural and homemaking exhibits. Palmer is also the site of the Midsummer Festival in June, featuring the Scottish Games Championships, the Grotto Lunkers competition, a horse show, and the Miss Matanuska Valley Pageant.

As you drive through this fertile valley, you'll see miles of cultivated fields, dairies and a creamery, poultry farms, and fine homes and barns—connected by a network of roads.

A weekend retreat for Anchorage residents, the Palmer-Wasilla-Big Lake area contains numerous state campgrounds, resorts, and roads leading to fishing, hunting, boating, water skiing, and sailing vacation spots.

Any trip to the Matanuska Valley should include a stop at the old Indian village of Eklutna, 26 miles from Anchorage. Visit Old St. Nicholas Russian Orthodox Church (another frame church, built in 1962, is nearby but not as interesting to visit) and the Indian burial ground with its "spirit houses." These colorfully painted miniature houses are placed over graves to hold the spirits of the deceased and to protect their possessions. Crosses in front of the spirit house indicate conversions to the Russian Orthodox faith. Contributions go to restoring the church and maintaining the property.

Side trip to Mt. Alyeska and Portage Glacier

Fifty miles of the Seward Highway winds southeast along the Turnagain Arm of Cook Inlet. Near the point where Glacier Creek flows into the arm are Girdwood, site of an old rail station, and Mt. Alyeska, a year-round resort.

Skiers challenge the slopes during winter; a major summertime attraction is the 1¼-mile double chair lift.

The panoramic view from the sundeck and restaurant at the top of the lift leaves you breathless. You look out from above timberline onto spruce-wooded slopes below, over cliffs and waterfalls, to beautiful Girdwood Valley and the waters of Turnagain Arm.

Smoothly rolling alpine meadows abound with colorful wildflowers. Eight glaciers are cradled among mountain peaks.

Down below, Alyeska Resort offers accommodations for 200, an attractive restaurant and lounge, gift store, ski shop with school and equipment rentals. Alyeska, Alaska's largest ski area, offers glacier skiing and lighted slopes for night skiing.

Of interest nearby is a working gold mine where you can try your hand at panning. Browse through a couple of interesting shops: Alaska Seal Oil Candle Co. and Kobuk Valley Jade Co. (items are produced from nephrite jade found above the Arctic Circle).

At the head of Turnagain Arm, on a 6-mile spur from the main road at Portage, is the turnoff for Portage Glacier, three campgrounds, and a visitor center. The road ends at iceberg-choked Portage Lake. Until 1913 the glacier's face ended where the parking lot is today. Now the glacier is in retreat; its present position is almost 2 miles away.

Forest Service naturalists are on hand at the visitor center in summer to explain the many natural features of the Portage Glacier Recreation Area. A hiking trail leads up the valley from the right of the center. During July and August, watch salmon spawning in nearby Portage Creek.

To Prince William Sound

Sixty miles southeast of Anchorage lies Prince William Sound, a saltwater bay protected by rugged cliffs and punctuated by forested islands. This is the home of Columbia Glacier, a mammoth mass of ice 41 miles long and over 4 miles wide, with a 300-foot-high face.

For a most rewarding excursion from Anchorage, be sure to include a cruise on Prince William Sound by sightseeing boat or ferry. Access to the sound is through the port cities of Whittier or Valdez.

Getting to Whittier. No highway leads to this small seaport. During summer, Alaska Railroad operates the Iceworm, a daily train with flat cars on which buses, cars, and campers travel piggyback from Portage rail station. Passengers and vehicles go by rail through two tunnels to Whittier.

Getting to Valdez. The only Prince William Sound community connecting with the state's highway system is Valdez, at the south terminus of the Richardson Highway (see page 76). Valdez is also the southern terminus of the 800-mile-long Alaska pipeline. Sightseeing excursions rest overnight here.

Dubbed the "Switzerland of Alaska," Valdez was hard-hit by the 1964 earthquake. When the town was rebuilt, it was moved four miles to a new and better site. Now it has a fine boat harbor and docks for ships and ferries. Quake-damaged roads were rebuilt.

The oil era has strained accommodations in this small city. If you are traveling on your own, be sure to have advance reservations. Several attractive campgrounds in the area sport their own private waterfalls.

Puerto de Valdez, a beautiful fiord in Prince William Sound, was given its name by a Spanish explorer in 1790. A settlement sprang up in 1898 on a terminal moraine at the head of the fiord. From there, gold stampeders crossed formidable glaciers and mountains to reach the gold fields. As Fairbanks boomed in the 1900s, Valdez became its supply port. Supplies were then hauled 365 miles over the Valdez Trail (now the Richardson Highway) by dog teams and horses in winter; later the trail was improved so wagons could be used.

You can reach Valdez by car or bus from Anchorage or Fairbanks; by ferry from Cordova and, in the summertime, from Whittier; or by Polar and AAI airlines.

The cruise. The *Glacier Queen*, a sightseeing boat, makes one round-trip daily between Valdez and Whittier, inching audaciously up to the face of Columbia Glacier to give its passengers a good look at giant slabs of ice breaking loose and thundering down into the sea. (Don't be discouraged if it's overcast or raining; the glacier looks even more blue under gray skies.)

Amphibious plane *at rest between stands of aspen is typical transport of modern "frontier days."*

At Eklutna, *near Anchorage, Indian spirit houses protect the treasured possessions of departed souls; Russian crosses are distinguished by the slant of the third and lowest arm.*

The crew nets glacial ice for your midday cocktail while you watch seals drying off on ice floes and listen to gulls screech as they dive for fish. En route, you may see porpoises or whales.

Advance reservations are necessary for the *Glacier Queen* cruise; check with a travel agent or Westours.

The ferry *Bartlett* operates daily, except Tuesday and Thursday, during the summer between Whittier, Valdez, and Cordova. The Whittier-Valdez segment takes about 7 hours. The *Tustumena* ferryliner connects Seward on the Kenai Peninsula with Valdez and Cordova. You can drive to Seward (about 130 miles from Anchorage), board the ferry, and arrive in Valdez about 12 hours later. For information on the Southwest Ferry System, write to the Department of Transportation and Public Facilities, Division of Marine Highway Systems, Pouch R, Juneau, AK 99811.

Though ferries don't give as close or long a look at Columbia Glacier as the sightseeing boat does, they do pause so you can see and hear this active tidewater glacier.

Cordova. The small community of Cordova retains a delightful flavor of old Alaska. Now off the beaten track, it is reached by air or by ferry from Valdez and, in the summertime, from Whittier. When completed, the Copper River Highway will intersect the Richardson Highway south of Thompson Pass.

Once a lusty, brawling railroad and mining terminal, Cordova was the setting for Rex Beach's *Iron Trail*. This novel is an account of the building of the Copper River Railroad to the rich copper deposits of Kennicott, which produced more than $100 million before being abandoned in 1938.

Sportsmen come to Cordova for the good fishing (salt or fresh water) and hunting in season. The town is located near the mouth of the Copper River, scene of famed salmon runs. The Copper River Mud Flats teem with ducks, geese, and swans. In addition to the commercial salmon industry, clam and crab canneries operate busily. Boats and planes are available for charter; in winter, skiing is a popular sport here. The annual Iceworm Festival takes place in February.

The Kenai Peninsula

This huge chunk of land that jabs like a fat thumb south from Anchorage into the Gulf of Alaska is a perfect destination for sportfishing, clamming, camping, canoeing, sailing, hiking, berrypicking, birding, or just getting off the beaten path.

The ruggedly beautiful, untracked interior of this peninsula is still wild enough to get lost in.

But along the coast, old Russian fishing villages and new oil boom towns have begun to develop facilities for an increasing number of visitors.

To the southeast, the ice-scoured Kenai Mountains drop straight down into deep glacial fiords. To the west, rolling tundra plains, covered with a light stand of aspen and birch, slope down to graceful ribbons of beach along Cook Inlet.

A frontier feeling lingers. Scattered families still live in hand-hewn log cabins. You can still see signs of the first settlers who came in 1791; the Russians established their second permanent Alaskan colony in what is now the town of Kenai. Small homesteads and truck gardens abound in the coastal vicinity of Kenai and Homer, Alaska's fishing and canning centers.

Even though the Kenai Peninsula is close enough to Anchorage to be sampled easily in a day, a variety of activities could keep you busy for a whole vacation.

Getting to the Kenai

From Anchorage, Wien Air Alaska and Alaska Aeronautical Industries (AAI) offer scheduled service to Seward, Kenai, and Homer. Transportation Services operates scheduled motorcoach service between Anchorage and Seward. Several companies offer tour packages.

Rental cars, trucks, and campers are available for the motorist from Anchorage. The Seward-Anchorage Highway (State Highway 1) heads southeast from Anchorage to the turnoff to Portage Glacier, then swings southwest into the Kenai Peninsula, where it divides. State 9 continues south to Seward, and State 1 turns west to become the Sterling Highway. Both highways are paved; most towns have gas stations, stores, restaurants, and lodging.

From Anchorage to Seward

The Portage Glacier detour (about 50 miles from Anchorage) gives you a chance to take a close-up look at this giant field of ice. Huge ice blocks break off the slowly receding glacier and float majestically across Portage Glacier toward the visitor center.

After the turnoff to Portage Glacier, State 1 gradually climbs up into Turnagain Pass through impressive forests. You pass open meadows

(Continued on page 78)

Glacier Queen puts audaciously up to face of Columbia Glacier in Prince William Sound.

Scenic Richardson Highway

The drive from the interior to the coast takes you into ruggedly beautiful mountains, over two passes, through the lovely Copper River Valley, and alongside an impressive glacier. Midway along the route is a connection with the Glenn Highway to Anchorage.

The Richardson Highway is Alaska's first road. Originally a pack trail for gold seekers in the late 1800s, trafficked with wagons, snowshoes, and dog sleds in winter, the trail was gradually upgraded. Today it is a modern paved highway.

Along its route you pass by interesting rock formations, view tundra meadows, wind through tunnels and alongside rivers and cascading waterfalls.

Highway grades are well engineered. Even motorists pulling trailers will have no trouble.

Start of the highway. The paved Richardson Highway branches off the Alaska Highway at Delta Junction, 98 miles from Fairbanks. It ends at Valdez on Prince William Sound. For most of the way along the road, you'll be traveling the same route as the Alaska pipeline.

At its start, the highway crosses a huge terminal moraine before dropping down to the Delta River, which pours out of the Alaska Range.

Eleven miles past Donnelly Creek State Campground, you look west to Black Rapids Glacier—dubbed the "galloping glacier" in 1936–37 when it made a sudden and dramatic advance of several miles, moving as much as 25 feet a day.

Isabell Pass. You follow the river toward Isabell Pass (3,310 feet), with bare, rocky, ragged mountains on either side. Near the pass a side road goes to Fielding Lake, a popular camping and fishing spot. From the highway you'll be able to see Gulkana Glacier and Summit Lake.

At the summit of Isabell Pass is a historical marker honoring General Wilds P. Richardson, first president of the Alaska Road Commission, for whom the highway is named. The road follows the lake's outlet river; you can watch salmon spawning in season. In the fall you may see caribou in this area.

Around Paxson. Originally roadhouses were built one day's stagecoach ride apart for the travelers' convenience. Some of these way stations remain; one is the original Paxson's Roadhouse near a modern lodge with a similar name. This area offers good hunting and fishing.

At Paxson, the Denali Highway branches off to Mt. McKinley National Park. South of here the Richardson Highway parallels Paxson Lake (known for good fishing).

Eighteen miles south of Paxson is Sourdough Roadhouse, oldest existing roadhouse in Alaska, still operating in the original building. It was once a stopping place for weary dog mushers and teamsters. Sourdough breakfast is served anytime.

Copper Center. At Gulkana Junction you join the Glenn Highway for 14 miles. At Glennallen, the Glenn Highway heads west toward Anchorage; the Richardson Highway continues south to Copper Center, an old settlement dating back to gold rush days. Today it consists of a post office, store, and a few scattered residences.

One mile before reaching Copper Center, the highway passes through the original Copper Indian village and native school. Copper Center was the site of the first homestead in southcentral Alaska. Its trading post (now modernized) was established in 1896. The Copper Center Lodge was selected by the Centennial Commission as one of 30 sites of historical importance in Alaska.

Highway to Chitina and McCarthy. A few miles farther south is Willow Lake, mirroring on clear days the towering, glacier-frosted peaks of the Wrangell Range. Past the lake the Richardson Highway intersects the Edgerton Highway (mostly a poor road) which goes to Chitina, a tired old town with a new lodge.

Chitina. Chitina was a lusty, brawling camp from the early 1900s, when a railroad was built to haul copper concentrates from the rich Kennecott mines, until 1938, when both railroad and mines stopped operations.

Travelers come today to view the deserted, tumble-down buildings. You'll find a hotel and restaurant.

Campgrounds are located beside Trout Lake in downtown Chitina and on the McCarthy side of the Copper River bridge. Fishing is good, with abundant salmon runs in the Copper River.

Sobek Expeditions Inc. (P. O. Box 67, Angels Camp, CA 95222) operates 7-day river trips on the Copper past half a dozen major glaciers, several of which "calve" directly into the river. The river is big, fast, and milky with glacial debris. It provides a swiftly moving ride past some of North America's largest peaks.

McCarthy and Kennicott. The Edgerton Highway goes on to McCarthy (check for washed-out bridges) for a venture into the wilderness.

Dependent on the nearby Kennecott Copper Mine, McCarthy flourished from the turn-of-the-century until the mine and railway were abandoned in 1938.

Camper *with trailer enters cavernous interior of ferry docked at Valdez.*

Today, McCarthy has a handful of residents, a couple of stores (including a gas pump), and an unsurfaced airstrip.

Kennicott, 4 miles away, nestles in spectacular mountain and glacier country. Abandoned mine buildings spill down hillsides that once yielded about $175 million in copper ore.

The Kennecott Lodge offers vacation packages, featuring tours of the ghost town and mine, along with camping and horseback riding. For information, check at the old grocery store in McCarthy for horse-and-buggy transportation to the lodge or check at the Ahtna Lodge in Glennallen for daily summer flights.

Old relics of mining days are still in evidence, but visitors are asked to leave them untouched; the town is privately owned.

Near Valdez. Back on the Richardson Highway, you come to the Tonsina Lodge, a two-story log building erected during gold rush days. It was one of the first to have "inside plumbing."

The entire Copper River Valley is scenic—the snow-covered Wrangell Mountains form a backdrop above old river-cut gravel terraces. Leaving the valley, you climb toward Thompson Pass (2,722 feet), passing beaver dams, and on to Worthington Glacier.

You begin a rapid descent from the pass, 25 miles from Valdez. Numerous campgrounds abound, and spectacular waterfalls cascade over magnificent rock formations (Horsetail and Bridal Veil among the best). In Keystone Canyon you'll see an old hand-cut tunnel made during the early days when there was a plan to build a railroad.

In Valdez. Moved to its present location (4 miles from its original site) after the 1964 earthquake, Valdez (pronounced "val DEEZ") is a modern city. The supply of accommodations and facilities can hardly keep up with the pressures of the little town's boom. It now stands at the terminus of the Alaska pipeline.

Even blemished by storage tanks, oil freighters, and sections of pipe, the town's surroundings are impressive. Often called the "Switzerland of Alaska," its beautiful fiord and towering snow-carved mountains attract the eye. Valdez' small boat harbor is crowded with pleasure crafts.

Miners and packers founded the turn-of-the-century community so they could reach the gold fields of Fairbanks. Its present frenzied activity is not unlike that of the gold rush era.

Good salmon catch rewards this commercial fisherman on cold waters of Kenai Peninsula.

…Continued from page 74

color-splashed in summer with false azalea, wild rose, violets, and several types of berries.

The turnoff to Hope, almost a ghost town, is about 12 miles beyond the pass. In 1896, about 2,500 prospectors poured into Hope and nearby Sunrise in Kenai's big gold rush. Though the rush was short-lived, a few mines kept producing, and a few sourdoughs drifted in to work them.

You can try your hand at panning at Resurrection Creek. Turn off the 17-mile gravel road to Hope onto Resurrection Pass Trail road a mile before town.

Back on State 1, it's 20 more miles to the junction with the Sterling Highway at Tern Lake, named for the Arctic terns nesting here each summer. State 9 climbs up over Moose Pass, then gradually winds down to Seward through spectacular mountains and past good trout fishing lakes and streams. You need a fishing license before you cast a line.

Seward, 128 miles from Anchorage, nestles between Resurrection Bay and hulking Mt. Marathon. This scenic town suffered extensive earthquake and tidal wave damage in 1964. Rebuilt since then, Seward is a thriving port and favorite boating and fishing spot for Anchorage residents.

This lovely harbor has long been the main Alaska Railroad port. Founded in 1903 as a starting point for the Alaska Central Railroad, the town was named for William H. Seward, U.S. Secretary of State who negotiated for the Alaska purchase. The railroad was to have been built to tap the Matanuska Valley coal fields. But it was not until 1923, nine years after the U.S. government took over the project, that the railroad to Matanuska and Fairbanks was completed.

In 1793, here at Resurrection Bay, Alexander Baranof built and launched the *Phoenix*—first ship built in Alaska. Today, you will find boats to charter for sportfishing, visiting Rugged Island's sea lions, or viewing bird rookeries on other islands.

Hotels, motels, a city campground, and a large camping area by the small boat harbor hold visitors who come to see the annual foot race up 3,000-foot Mt. Marathon on July 4 or to participate in the annual Silver Salmon Derby, an 8-day, around-the-clock event in mid-August.

Except for Seward, all of the peninsula along the Anchorage-Seward Highway is part of the Chugach National Forest. You will find many Forest Service campgrounds and numerous trail systems. For a detailed map and information on the area, write to Forest Supervisor, Chugach National Forest, 121 W. Fireweed Lane, Suite 205, Anchorage, AK 99503.

The Sterling Highway

From its junction with the Seward Highway, the Sterling Highway runs 135 miles to Homer. You'll come upon a dozen or more motels, lodges, and hunting and fishing camps along the way.

The highway starts in rocky, mountainous country where you have a good chance of seeing Dall sheep along the face of the mountains. Look high.

When you leave the Chugach National Forest, you're in moose country. Here, in the lowlands, thick stands of spruce, birch, and aspen hide hundreds of tiny lakes and streams that offer food and protection for these ungainly members of the deer family. This is the Kenai National Moose Range.

Kenai National Moose Range

Set aside by Presidential order in 1941, the Kenai National Moose Range is a wildlife refuge encompassing 1.7 million acres. Established to preserve representative native wildlife species—in particular the largest antlered animal on earth—the range provides habitat for moose, brown and black bear, Dall sheep, and mountain goat.

Rainbow, Dolly Varden, lake trout, and spawning salmon inhabit most of the waters. A variety of birds—including ptarmigan, loons, and the rare trumpeter swan—nest here.

The range is a popular recreational area, offering fishing, boating, hiking, camping, and picnicking in the summer; ice-fishing, cross-country skiing, dog-sledding, snowshoeing, and snowmobiling in the winter.

Probably the most interesting feature of the moose range is the Kenai Canoe Trails. Varying in difficulty from "beginner" to "expert," the trails wind through the northern part of the range along rivers or lakes connected by short portages. Both trails begin near the community of Sterling.

Swanson River Canoe Route is the largest; about 80 miles of waterways link more than 40 lakes with about 46 miles of river. An average trip, canoeing the river and a portion of the lakes, takes about a week; for a shorter trip you can just sample a few lakes and then backtrack.

The Swan Lake Canoe Route is better suited to Alaska visitors who won't be using a car but have come prepared for wilderness camping. The entire system offers roughly 60 miles of canoeing, connecting 30 lakes with the Moose River.

You need only 3 to 5 days to sample about a third of the lakes and approximately 25 miles of the Moose River. You end your trip back at your starting point—the Moose River bridge on State 1.

Preparing for a trip is not difficult. You can rent an aluminum canoe, paddles, and life jackets. For a fee, outfitters will shuttle you, your equip-

ment, and your canoe to the head of Swan Lake Canoe Route.

If you take the Swanson River Route, you can arrange to be picked up at the end of your trip.

Boaters with their own equipment should check for current information on water conditions. Information and detailed maps are available by writing to the Kenai National Moose Range, Box 500, Kenai, AK 99611.

The road to the trailhead of the Swanson River Route is well marked; canoe trails are not marked as clearly. Several portages are almost hidden.

Travel light. Possible wave splash and a good chance of summer rain indicate need for waterproof packs, rain ponchos, a tent, and a campstove. Cans and bottles have no place in the wilderness. Over-burdened canoes are unsafe—stow packs in the bottom of the canoe and tie them to the boat.

Of all the wild animals you are likely to encounter, a cow moose with a calf is the most unpredictable. Watch from a safe distance; don't approach a lone calf and don't come between a calf and its mother. The most bothersome of Alaska's wildlife is the lowly mosquito. Lay in a good supply of repellent.

Before setting off on your canoe adventure, be sure you have confirmed reservations for transportation, accommodations, and equipment.

Along the highway to Homer

This route passes through a number of small, but intriguing, villages. Each is worth a stop or a short visit.

Soldotna, about 55 miles west of the junction of State Highways 1 and 9, is itself a junction point. Turn right to Kenai, or stay on Sterling Highway 78 miles to Homer. Soldotna is a new oil town in the heart of promising fishing and hunting country. It has every facility you're likely to need, including a shopping center.

Kenai, on the shore of Cook Inlet, was founded in 1791 as a Russian fur trading post. Today Kenai boasts the oldest Russian Orthodox church left in Alaska—the Church of the Assumption of the Virgin Mary, built around 1896. A log barracks in restored Fort Kenay (1846 U.S. military post) contains a historical museum.

A fast-growing city because of oil and gas discoveries, Kenai is a center for canoe trips, bush flights, and clam digging. Clam Gulch, about 18 miles out of Soldotna on the Sterling Highway, is one of the easily accessible beaches along the Cook Inlet. You can dig for razor clams during low tide. Clamming shovels can be rented here.

Across Cook Inlet from Kenai, four active volcanoes are visible. These are part of the Pacific "ring of fire," the earth's most active seismic zone. About forty more active volcanoes rise in the Aleutian Range.

Photogenic Ninilchik's Russian church and neat cemetery on top of the hill behind town face Cook Inlet; on a clear day you can see the Chigmit Mountains across the inlet.

Descendants of the Russian fur traders still live here. Now a fishing village, Ninilchik offers an unexcelled old-world setting with quaint fishing shacks and log homes. Inhabitants still speak their native tongue.

This is gently rolling forest land, interspersed with open meadows and active trout streams. Several of the streams—Ninilchik River, Deep Creek, and Anchor River—also have open periods for king salmon fishing. Be sure to get a special punch card with your license.

Anchor Point, a small highway community, is located as far west as you can drive on the North American continent. Captain Cook, searching for the famed Northwest Passage, anchored here. The campground may be crowded during salmon season.

Homer – an artist's delight

The early Russians who visited the Cook Inlet side of the lower Kenai Peninsula called this region "Summerland" for good reason. Protected from the Gulf of Alaska storms by the towering ice-capped Kenai Range, this area enjoys a mild climate with an average rainfall of 25 inches.

In summer the wildflowers—lupine and fireweed predominating—are a particular delight on hills and fields around town. And in the fall, after the first frosts have come, the fireweed turns red, and the birches, poplars, and aspens glimmer with gold, reminding you of Indian summer.

Moose *and her calf cautiously eye photographer and camera through a thick stand of spruce.*

Standing *stark and simple against Cook Inlet and a vast gray sky, Russian "old believers" church overlooks Ninilchik.*

All about glaciers

In spite of Alaska's reputation as a land of cold and snow, less than 5% of the state is encased in ice, and that small percentage holds unique and rewarding vistas for travelers. Though the percentage of ice is low, the land locked beneath perennial ice covers over 28,000 square miles—and includes more than half the world's glaciers. Malaspina Glacier, near Yakutat, is larger than Switzerland.

This phenomenon of frozen and compressed water is located conveniently for visitors in the southcentral and southeastern parts of the state; the interior and north are relatively arid. It takes water to make ice, and the maritime climate of southern Alaska provides it in abundance. Extraordinary snowfall, at times exceeding 400 inches annually, provides the seed of glaciation.

If the annual snowfall exceeds the melt rate, a buildup occurs. However, this buildup can take place without forming a glacier. Key ingredients for glacial formation seem to be time and pressure. Over the years, the weight of snow and ice cause lower ice layers to metamorphose into a crystal formation unique to glacial ice. These crystals, having a plastic or flexible tendency, enable a mass of ice to flow slowly downhill.

The ice also takes on a pronounced blue coloring due to compaction, more pronounced on overcast days than in brilliant sunlight.

Large glaciers do a lot of earth-moving as they flow, literally creating landscapes. Glaciers are responsible for the spectacular U-shaped valleys of the western Sierras (such as Yosemite), the sharp peaked ridges of the northern Cascades in Washington, and the dramatic fiords of Scandinavia and Alaska. A glacial advance thousands of years ago helped grind down an ancient mountain range in eastern Canada, creating that area's great plains.

If you are flying over a glacier, there are some basic features to look for. The most pronounced are called *moraines*.

Moraines consist of rock and dirt picked up by the glacier as it slides downhill. Lateral and medial moraines are seen as dark bands running the length of the glacier, like dark lines on a white highway. Terminal moraines are rock and debris bulldozed by the glacier, found at its toe.

Crevasse fields are also apparent. A crevasse is a major fracture in the glacier's surface. A large field of these fractures indicates that the glacier is undergoing some stress, probably riding over a hill or into a "fall" below.

Ogives, rarer and more subtle than moraines or crevasses, are wave patterns generally formed at the base of the glacier as it slowly surges over extreme declinations in its bed.

Visitors to Alaska will see three types of glaciers: valley glaciers in any of the coastal mountain ranges and the Alaska Range; piedmont glaciers (flowing onto a plain) along the southcentral coast; and tidewater glaciers in Prince William Sound and throughout Southeast Alaska.

Tidewater glaciers provide one of nature's most dramatic spectacles. These glaciers, ending in the sea, are easily approached by boat, and the visitor can safely move in relatively close.

The faces of some of these glaciers can reach 600 feet high. Enormous pieces of ice, some thousands of years old, "calve" into the sea with thundering reports. The falling ice sends up great waves, and resulting icebergs take on beautifully sculpted shapes.

Scheduled excursions are offered to Columbia Glacier (largest tidewater glacier in North America) in Prince William Sound near Anchorage, to Le Conte Glacier near Petersburg, and to several awesome glaciers in Glacier Bay National Monument.

Homer, often called Alaska's Cape Cod, lies at the end of the Sterling Highway, on the shore of Kachemak Bay. Homesteads and homesites border the town on the land side. Many of those on a bluff overlooking the bay command a fine view of the Kenai Range. Moose and bear are frequent visitors.

A half-dozen glaciers flank the horizon to the east. You see them as you approach town on Skyline Drive. There's an even better view from East Road. Such vistas attracted the colony of artists who live and work here.

Early-day residents easily lived off the land. There were moose and mountain sheep; a profusion of wild berries; clams on the beach; and king crabs, halibut, and salmon in Kachemak Bay. After a storm, Homer residents could pick up coal on the beaches. A few settlers saw the agricultural possibilities and took up homesteads, but it was not until a road was punched through that a real wave of homesteaders arrived.

Homer Spit

A long, narrow, natural sand bar jutting almost five miles into the bay is the site of Homer Pennock's original gold-prospecting town, which burned when an exposed coal seam caught fire.

Clustered around the end of the spit are a small boat harbor, seafood restaurants, hotel, campground, seafood plants, boat charter and building firms, and a number of small shops. The ferry M/V *Tustumena* docks here. You can visit Homer's Salty Dawg Saloon, one of two original buildings to survive both the big fire of 1907 and the 1964 earthquake.

You board a fishing boat for a cruise of Kachemak Bay, visiting Gull Island—a raucous sea bird rookery—and Halibut Cove, where you walk to an artist's studio and enjoy complimentary refreshments.

Downtown, the Pratt Museum features Russian, Indian, and Aleut artifacts, a collection of early-day tools and utensils, and wildlife dioramas. At Alaska Wild Berry Products, you can sample some of the many tasty jams, jellies,

and candies made from berries. Each year, the plant processes Alaskan wild berries picked by local people throughout the state for gift packages sent all over the world.

Homer celebrates the harvest with a display of local agricultural products at the August fair. In February, residents hold a winter carnival.

Some local artists (including wildflower painter Toby Tyler) have downtown studios. Norman Lowell, a fine landscape painter, is located at Anchor Point; Diana Tillion, who paints with sepia (octopus ink), lives across the bay at Halibut Cove.

One tour operator offers regularly scheduled one and two-day sightseeing packages to Homer and Kachemak Bay.

If you're on your own, be sure to have confirmed overnight accommodations during the busy summer months. You'll find a handful of hotels and motels plus several good restaurants and supper clubs.

Around Kachemak Bay

The name *Kachemak* in Aleut means "smoky bay"; it probably derives from the smoldering coal seams which long ago smoked along the shores of the bay. The erosion of these bluffs (particularly near Anchor Point) create a plentiful supply of winter fuel for residents.

The magnificent deepwater bay reaches inland from Cook Inlet for 30 miles, with an average width of 7 miles. The wild, timbered coastline across from Homer is indented with fiords and inlets poking far into the rugged glacier-capped peaks of the Kenai Mountains.

Several air taxi operators and a helicopter service offer charters for flightseeing, sportfishing, hunting, camping, clam digging, or photography. They'll fly you to the McNeil River to watch brown bear fishing or to Iliamna Lake, on the Alaska Peninsula, to angle for rainbow trout. Some of the best scenic excursions cruise around Kachemak Bay.

Visiting a glacier that spills down from the Harding Icefield across the bay makes a fascinating flight. The largest and most spectacular of these glaciers is Grewingk Glacier in Kachemak Bay State Park—named by an explorer in honor of a German geologist who had published work on Alaskan volcanism. A long gravel bar called Glacier Spit at its terminal morraine, makes a popular outing for charter plane or boat.

Seldovia, a colorful fishing village across Kachemak Bay from Homer, is accessible by once-a-week ferry or by daily air flights (weather permitting). Though the 1964 earthquake dropped Seldovia several feet, the damaged area has been rebuilt. Board sidewalks built on pil-

Campers line distant Homer Spit at end of Kenai Peninsula. Natural gravel finger extends 5 miles into Kachemak Bay.

ings are lined with canneries, stores, restaurants, and waterfront houses.

Seldovia is home port for salmon and king crab fishing boats. Wakefield Fisheries crab processing plant (open for touring) is Alaska's most modern.

Two other stops possible by air are Port Graham, a native village, and English Bay, noted for good fishing.

Kachemak Bay Wilderness Lodge, accessible only by boat, float plane, or helicopter (at low tide), is a good example of Alaskan bush living. At this small, family-run operation, you can go fishing, hiking, or boating. A restful sauna near your cabin and home-cooked meals at the main lodge greet you in the evening. For information on this lodge at the edge of Kachemak Bay Wilderness Park, write to Mike and Diane McBride, China Poot Bay via Homer, AK 99603.

Refreshing rest stop, *the Salty Dawg Saloon on Homer Spit has held together for 75 years, its heavy log walls surviving fire and earthquake.*

Bush pilots –Alaska's "bird men"

As any resident will tell you, you haven't really seen Alaska until you leave the highways and take to the air. More people have pilot's licenses in Alaska than in any other state. The reason is purely practical: distances are great and settlements can often be reached only by light plane.

Air travel is easy to arrange. Several airlines provide scheduled service to various points around the state. In addition, numerous air taxis (operated by "bush pilots") travel to outlying areas.

Why are they called bush pilots? The answer is fairly obvious. They fly to remote areas in the back country where no scheduled service (or often even an airstrip) exists.

Because of their daring feats, great legends have embellished the reputation of Alaska's "bird men."

But for all their romance, bush pilots are a variable lot. Don't take the first name you see advertised in the Yellow Pages.

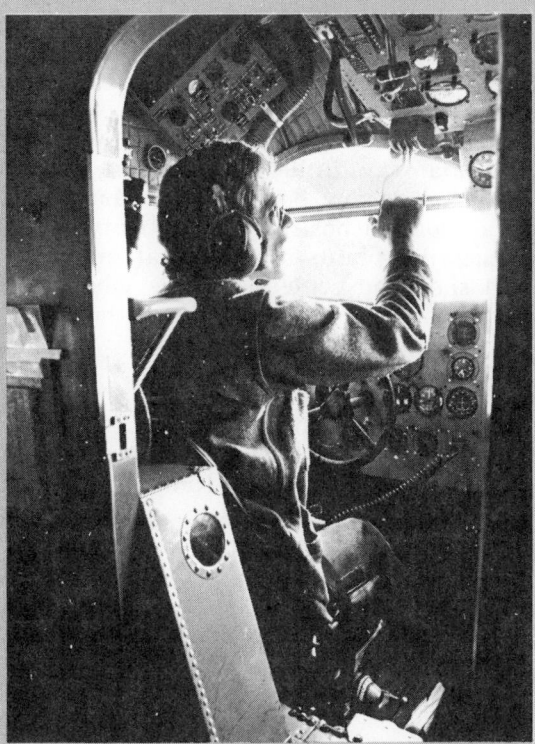

In amphibious *Gruman Goose, you can watch both scenery and pilot.*

Shop around. Rates vary—and so does experience. In some areas you'll find only one flight service; large population centers such as Anchorage and Fairbanks give you a wider choice.

Planes also come in various shapes and sizes. You could find yourself in a turbo jet or a prop plane; the craft will have wheels for conventional strips, pontoons for watery landings, and skis for ice fields.

In some cases you will discover that chartering a plane can be as inexpensive as taking a commercial airline—and even more convenient.

A good way to cut costs is to plan your trip to coincide with a drop or pickup the pilot is already scheduled to make. You pay only for your additional stop, and you may have the opportunity to fly a scenic route. Naturally, the more people to share a charter, the less expensive it is for each individual.

Fishermen use bush pilots to fly to remote lakes or rivers. Hunters fly where the game is.

Some of the most scenic areas for a charter flight are Southeast Alaska, the glacier country, Mt. McKinley, or remote sections of the Arctic.

The Southwest Corner

Southwest of Anchorage lies a 40,000-square-mile region with only 4,000 population. This is the Bristol Bay country, laced with five important rivers that display the greatest red salmon run in the world. The rivers' names read like a series of sneezes—Kvichak, Nushagak, Naknek, Ugashik, and Egegik.

At one time 24 canneries operated in the bay area. Rex Beach worked in one of them in the 1900s, gathering material for his novel *The Silver Horde*. Canneries still rumble busily with activity, and visitors are welcome.

Southwest Alaska also encompasses the islands of the Aleutian Chain, the Pribilof Islands, Kodiak Island (noted for its large brown bears), Katmai National Monument with its "Valley of Ten Thousand Smokes," and vast bird nesting regions in the deltas of the Kuskokwim and Yukon rivers.

You won't find crowds here or big cities, but you will discover a region of breathtaking natural beauty with miles of untracked valleys and unnamed rivers. At prime fishing spots, bears often outnumber people. Streams flash with silvery trout. Except for hotels in Kodiak and a lodge in Bethel, your accommodations will be rustic and your meals hearty, home-cooked fare.

Since no roads connect this region, the best way to get around Southwest Alaska is by air. You can reach Kodiak Island by ferry. From Anchorage, sightseeing packages are available to Kodiak, Katmai, and the Pribilofs. Prices include air fare, transfers, sightseeing, and lodging. Meals are extra (and expensive).

Wien Air Alaska flies daily to Kodiak, Katmai, and Bethel from Anchorage. Western Airlines offers direct service to Kodiak from Seattle. Reeve Aleutian Airways serves the Pribilof Islands by way of Cold Bay in the Aleutians.

Kodiak Island

This rugged island, ringed by its wind-swept coast, is famous for crabs growing to a spectacular size and for its huge brown bears. The city of Kodiak, largest of eight communities, nestles around an island-dotted bay. Bring your raincoat. Along with its mild climate, this lush green island experiences about 60 inches of rain yearly. On a clear day, however, your eye can feast on mountains, valleys, and coastline in a panorama rivaling few other Alaskan sites in scenic beauty.

Though damaged like Valdez by earthquake and tidal wave in 1964, the downtown section of Kodiak has now been rebuilt. You will find a small boat harbor, ferry dock, boatyard, seafood processing plants, and several modern stores and shopping centers. This is where you will want to sleep, eat, and drink on the island.

A Russian capital

Kodiak's name comes from the native word *Kikhatah*, meaning "island." As time passed, the word was pared down to Kadiak and finally became Kodiak.

Background mountains *rise from floor of Valley of Ten Thousand Smokes, Katmai National Monument.*

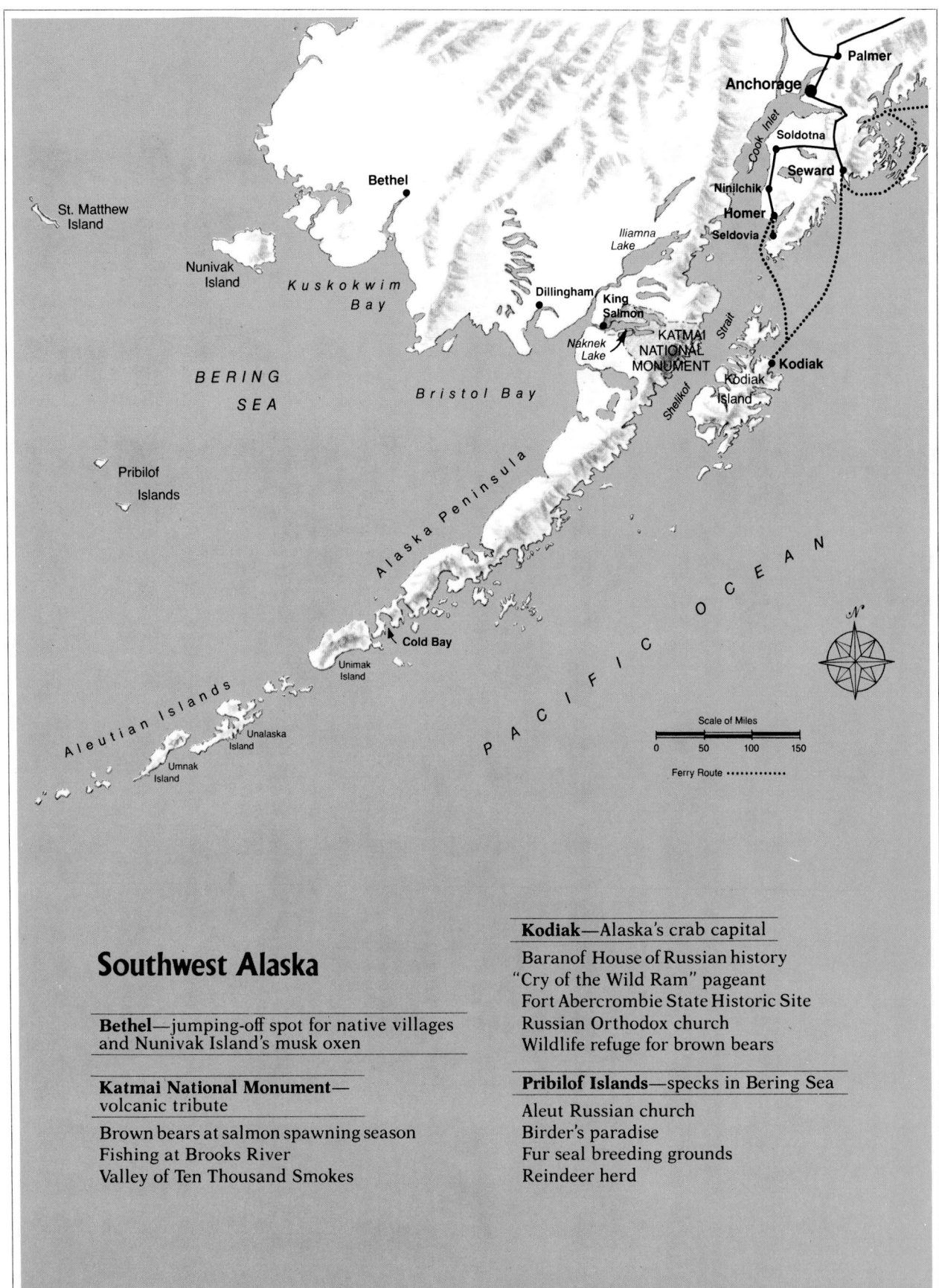

Map labels:
Palmer
Anchorage
Soldotna
Seward
Cook Inlet
Ninilchik
Homer
Seldovia
Iliamna Lake
Bethel
St. Matthew Island
Nunivak Island
Kuskokwim Bay
Dillingham
King Salmon
Naknek Lake
KATMAI NATIONAL MONUMENT
Strait
Kodiak
Kodiak Island
Shelikof
BERING SEA
Bristol Bay
Pribilof Islands
Alaska Peninsula
PACIFIC OCEAN
Cold Bay
Unimak Island
Aleutian Islands
Unalaska Island
Umnak Island

Scale of Miles
0   50   100   150

Ferry Route •••••••••••

Southwest Alaska

Bethel—jumping-off spot for native villages and Nunivak Island's musk oxen

Katmai National Monument—volcanic tribute

Brown bears at salmon spawning season
Fishing at Brooks River
Valley of Ten Thousand Smokes

Kodiak—Alaska's crab capital

Baranof House of Russian history
"Cry of the Wild Ram" pageant
Fort Abercrombie State Historic Site
Russian Orthodox church
Wildlife refuge for brown bears

Pribilof Islands—specks in Bering Sea

Aleut Russian church
Birder's paradise
Fur seal breeding grounds
Reindeer herd

The island is an intriguing place to visit. Discovered by a Russian explorer in 1673, it is the home of the oldest permanent European settlement in Alaska.

Russian fur traders and hunters established their first North American colony at Three Saints Bay on the south side of the island in 1784, but Baranof moved it in 1792 to the site of the present-day town of Kodiak. It remained the capital of Russian America until transferred to Sitka in 1804.

During the Katmai eruption, on nearby Alaska Peninsula, the island was covered with a black cloud of ash. When the cloud finally dissipated, Kodiak was buried under 18 inches of pumice. Roofs collapsed, wildlife suffered, and the fish—staple food of the natives—completely disappeared. Even today, the layer of ash can be seen under the moss on the trees.

The earthquake of 1964 that rolled through Alaska shook Kodiak, but it was the tidal wave that followed which virtually leveled the downtown area. The wave destroyed Kodiak's extensive fishing fleet and processing plants; lives were lost and many were left homeless.

How to get there

Air transportation to Kodiak is provided by Wien Air Alaska from Anchorage and by Western Airlines from Seattle. Kodiak Western Alaska Airlines serves Kodiak and outlying communities from Anchorage.

Amphibious air charters leave from the downtown bay. Rates are fairly high.

The Alaska State ferry M/V *Tustumena* serves Kodiak from Homer, Seldovia, Seward, Valdez, and Cordova. It also stops at Port Lions on the north side of Kodiak Island.

Accommodations

Kodiak's hotels fill up quickly during the summer months: make advance reservations. Both the Kodiak Travelodge and Shelikof Lodge have restaurants and lounges. A handful of good restaurants offer specialties ranging from Chinese food to filet mignon. Naturally, many menus feature fresh, local seafood.

Campgrounds are located at Fort Abercrombie State Park, north of town, and at Middle Bay, south of town. In addition, you'll find lots of other free scenic camping spots along the roads and beaches. A variety of stores accommodate most campers' requirements.

Kodiak National Wildlife Refuge

Flightseeing trips on local charter airlines reach the Kodiak National Wildlife Refuge. For information on the area, write to the refuge manager at Harbor View Bldg., Box 825, Kodiak, AK 99615.

Established in 1941 to preserve the natural habitat of the Kodiak bear, the refuge covers the southwestern two-thirds of the island.

Visitors to the refuge may catch sight of native red fox, land otter, weasel, brown bat, and other mammals in addition to the famous bear. Whales and porpoises sport in the estuaries, along with seals, sea otters, and sea lions.

Blacktail deer, reindeer, mountain goat, beaver, muskrat, mink snowshoe hare, red squirrel and marten were transplanted to Kodiak in the 1930s. Also look for Dall sheep and moose—introduced to the refuge more recently.

Of course, most visitors are curious about Kodiak bear. Approximately 2,400 of these tremendous animals inhabit the island. Males weigh up to 1,200 pounds.

Stories extoll their danger and ferocity, but most outdoorsmen find that bears avoid contact with man, lumbering away hurriedly as soon as they identify a human being. However, rare instances of unpredictable behavior do occur; keep a respectful distance from these large, powerful animals.

Summer, when the salmon swarm upstream, and early fall, when the berries are ripe, are the times of year when your chances are best of viewing these magnificent animals.

Waterfowl number in the millions along the 800 miles of coastline on the Kodiak refuge. You'll see duck, goose, swan, and quantities of bald eagle.

Kodiak is an outfitting point for hunters. For information, write to the Regional Director, Bureau of Sport Fisheries and Wildlife, P.O. Box 825, Kodiak, AK 99615.

Fishing

Fishing has long been the mainstay of Kodiak's economy. During the 1890s, 16-mile-long Karluk River was the greatest salmon-producing stream in the world. Today's large commercial fishing fleet hauls in catches of halibut, salmon, shrimp, and crab. The famous king crabs weigh up to 30 pounds and attain a 6-foot span. Every May, Kodiak holds a King Crab Festival.

You can walk along colorful cannery row where seafood is processed for export, sample it fresh from the ocean at one of Kodiak's seafood restaurants, or try your own luck with a rod. There's good sport fishing for Dolly Varden, steelhead, and salmon. You will need a boat or plane to reach the best fishing spots. Charter boats are not plentiful.

Afognak Island, 30 miles northwest of Kodiak,

Giant crabs *from waters around Kodiak weigh in at about 400 pounds per load.*

offers good remote hunting and fishing. Check with the U.S. Forest Service in Kodiak to reserve one of the four cabins on the island.

This is brown bear country. Both hikers and fishermen should make noise and carry a rifle for self-protection.

What to see

Visitors are welcome at the picturesque Russian Orthodox church with its onion-shaped domes. Either the priest or his wife will explain the icons and other religious works displayed inside. Ask about St. Herman, North America's first Russian Orthodox saint, who lived in Kodiak. Up the hill is a photogenic site—a neglected Russian cemetery.

The Baranof House, oldest building in Alaska, displays treasures from earlier days: antique Russian samovars, seal oil candles, jewelry, and Aleut basketry. The museum is open daily during the summer.

At Fort Abercrombie State Historic Site, 5 miles northeast of the city, explore grim ruins of World War II defenses. Kodiak was the center of a successful effort to dislodge the Japanese after their invasion of the Aleutians.

The fort has 12 campsites (each with pit toilet) scattered through the forest.

From Pillar Mountain, a 1,300-foot hill behind town, a winding road leads to an overlook where you get excellent views of Kodiak and other islands.

The island has a 55-mile road that offers an especially scenic drive on clear days. There are fossil beds and beaches for picnicking. Flight-seeing excursions take a closer look at Kodiak and other islands.

"Cry of the Wild Ram," a dramatized account of the first colony in Russian America and of Baranof, its leader, is presented by Kodiak residents each summer. An outdoor amphitheater on the shore of Monashka Bay provides a natural setting for the performance.

This historic play covers 15 years in the life of Alexander Baranof, governor of the Russian colony here.

If you are visiting Kodiak in August, plan to attend this event. It gives some fascinating insights into Russian colonial culture in Alaska.

Other summer festivals you might enjoy are the Great Buskin River Raft Race in September, St. Herman's Day in August, a Fourth of July celebration and carnival, and the Jaycee Rodeo and State Fair.

Wintertime festivities include a Harvest Ball, Christmas Bazaar and basketball tournament.

Kodiak U.S. Coast Guard Station, 6½ miles southwest of Kodiak, is one of the largest operational stations in the United States.

Woody Island, 2 miles east of Kodiak, marks some moments in history. It was a boatbuilding center and a port from which the Russians shipped ice to the California coast in the early and middle 1800s. Supposedly, Alaska's first horses were brought to Woody Island. Certainly, the first road in Alaska was built around the island. The settlement diminished as the population drifted to Kodiak.

Katmai National Monument

Famed for its Valley of Ten Thousand Smokes, Katmai National Monument stretches over more than 4,000 square miles. Second largest unit of the national park system, it is one of North America's great wilderness recreation areas. Once remote and largely undiscovered by visitors, today it is readily accessible from Anchorage by air.

The monument, established in 1918, covers a hundred miles of ocean bays, fiords, and lagoons, against a backdrop of glacier-covered peaks and volcanic crater lakes. Beyond the peaks lies a "wilderness within a wilderness"—forests, long lake chains, and the Valley of Ten Thousand Smokes.

History of an eruption

In June, 1912, Novarupta Volcano—then just a vent 6 miles east of Mt. Katmai—literally "blew its top" with a terrific explosion.

Before the eruption, the Katmai region was a land of tall grass, groves of trees, and scattered lakes. The series of events that changed the heart of it into a scene of barren desolation began with earthquakes, causing the natives to abandon their villages. Then the floor of the peaceful basin of the Ukak and Lethe rivers split into fissures at Novarupta, from which incandescent sand welled up on a cushion of escaping gases and flowed swiftly for 15 miles, covering everything in its path to depths as great as 300 feet.

Next the top of Mt. Katmai itself collapsed, perhaps from a subterranean outpouring of magma that emerged through Novarupta. Volcanic ash covered thousands of square miles.

The resulting dust cloud spread around the world, lowering temperatures over the entire northern hemisphere that year by blocking some of the sun's heat. A few years later, when scientists arrived to study the area, "ten thousand smokes" curled up from the valley to the west of the ragged stump of Mt. Katmai.

Later, deposits of ash and sand consolidated into tuff, a type of rock. (You'll see small pieces floating in the lakes.) There are fewer than a dozen smokes in the valley today, but the volcanoes around it still puff and rumble. During the past two decades, Mt. Trident has erupted four times, the last in 1969.

Since the eruption, the turbulent Ukak River has cut deep, narrow, polished gorges through the ash. Plant life is slowly returning. But this is a dynamic landscape; an eruption bringing major change could occur any time.

Wildlife and people

More than 30 species of land mammals have been observed at Katmai; the Alaska brown bear is the most prominent, in evidence from early spring until late fall. You'll find these bears feasting on wild berries or fishing the streams for spawning salmon. When you arrive at Katmai, a ranger meets you to explain precautions to take in the back country. Most trails were trod down by bears; when you're hiking, make plenty of noise to shoo them away.

Moose live in the coastal and lake regions, feeding on willows, water plants, and grasses. Smaller animals include the red fox, Arctic fox, wolf, lynx, and wolverine.

Waterfowl are abundant in the lakes region; some 40 species of songbirds can be observed during summer months. Even the rare bald eagle makes an occasional appearance. Sea lions and hair seals frequent rock outcroppings along the coast.

Accommodations and facilities

Wien Air Alaska provides accommodations and services at Brooks River and Lake Grosvenor.

Package tours from Anchorage are available from June to Labor Day. You transfer at King Salmon to floatplane and splash down at the lodge's front door.

Facilities at Brooks River Lodge on Naknek Lake include a modern lodge and cabins with plumbing. Meals are provided (at extra cost) in the lodge. Facilities at Lake Grosvenor Camp include a dining room and cabins with outside plumbing. You can rent fishing equipment and guide-operated boats at both locations.

At Brooks River the National Park Service maintains a campground with tables, water, wood, firepits, shelters, and food cache.

You may camp in the back country of the monument. Fire permits, required for camping, are issued at Brooks River Ranger Station or at the King Salmon headquarters.

Bring your camping supplies and groceries. Tents and stoves are for rent; fuel and some food are available at the small store. Campers can buy meals and scenic bus tour tickets at the lodge.

Weather

Come prepared for some sunshine and some stormy weather. Strong winds and sudden rainstorms, known as "williwaws," frequently sweep through the area. Bring comfortable clothing—a warm sweater or windbreaker, walking shoes or hiking boots, wool socks, and rain gear. You'll need insect repellent if you spend time near the water.

Activities

Fishing is probably the reason most people come to Katmai. Erudite fishermen say the Brooks River has some of the best salmon fishing in the world—and they would like to keep it a secret!

Each summer nearly a million salmon return to the Naknek river system to spawn after spending several years in ocean waters. You'll share fishing space along the river with bears.

Fishing is also good for rainbow trout, lake trout, Dolly Varden, grayling, whitefish, and northern pike. Silver, king, and humpback salmon are occasionally taken from the streams. You will need an Alaska fishing license to cast your line in the monument waters.

At Brooks River Lodge, Park Service ranger-naturalists lead walks and hikes and present evening programs to acquaint visitors with the monument. One of the easiest hikes follows a trail along the Brooks River, giving you a good look at the salmon jumping the falls on their way upstream to spawn.

Valley of Ten Thousand Smokes

A high point for first-time visitors to Katmai is an excursion to the Valley of Ten Thousand Smokes.

From the overlook, you gaze down upon some 40 square miles of valley, buried under 700 feet of volcanic debris, and across to snow-topped mountains. Pumice cliffs rise starkly from the valley floor along the meandering river.

Your scenic bus tour begins from the lodge early in the morning and takes you 23 miles to the valley's edge, stopping along the way for short walks or wildlife observation. After fording three streams, you reach Overlook Cabin. Now it's time for lunch (a box lunch is included in the price of this all-day excursion) or a hike into the valley.

Rangers lead hikes—about 2½ miles on a switchback trail. The climb back up is fairly steep: if you're not used to hiking, better remain at Overlook Cabin.

Back country hikes

Hikers and backpackers find that the Katmai offers some of the most exciting and rewarding wilderness experiences to be found anywhere. Though it's a rough and, at times, inhospitable country, it can give you the hiking trip of a lifetime—if you take reasonable precautions.

Late summer is the best time for hiking. The pesky mosquito is less bothersome, the terrain more stable.

The National Park Service provides plenty of information on hiking in the monument. A good guidebook to Katmai and its trail system is *Exploring Alaska's Katmai National Monument* (Alaska Travel Publications, Inc., Box 4-2031, Anchorage, AK 99509).

Out to the Aleutians

The Alaska Peninsula extends in a southwest crescent to form the Aleutian chain of islands pointing toward Kamchatka. This chain marks the dividing line between the North Pacific and the Bering Sea.

Called "Land of the Smoky Sea" by the natives, this is a treeless region of fog and wind, the birthplace of storms where the cold air from the north meets the warmth of the Japanese current. The area includes about 35 small, sparsely populated villages whose meager economy is based on fishing and some sheep and cattle raising.

At its farthest point, the Aleutian Chain is only one hour (by air) from Siberia, or 2 hours from Japan. It's surprisingly close to Hawaii—closer than any point on the California coast.

The semivolcanic archipelago of about 200 large islands and hundreds of smaller ones stretches over 1,000 miles from Unimak Island (closest to the Alaska mainland) to Attu Island, the most distant.

Though the Navy maintains extensive facilities at several locations, visitors are not encouraged. Places like Cold Bay (a stop on the way to the Pribilof Islands) abound with wildlife and waterfowl.

The Aleuts dominate the native population of this area. Skillful fishermen, in earlier times they often ventured far from shore in small light skin boats, searching for otters, seals, sea lions, and occasional whales.

Today most Aleuts fish commercially. Others go to Bristol Bay to work for the summer in canneries.

Izembek National Wildlife Range, a 320,000-acre waterfowl refuge near the tip of the Alaska Peninsula, attracts over 100 species of birds. Established to benefit the black brant, Izembek Lagoon has the world's largest eelgrass beds on which most of North America's brant feed during spring and fall migrations. Visitor access is via Cold Bay; facilities are very limited. Check with Reeve Aleutian Airways for more information.

Served by Reeve Aleutian Airways several times a week, the Aleutians are not a tourist destination. Facilities for overnight stays are practically nonexistent.

The Pribilof Islands

Several tiny dots of islands lie 200 miles north of the Aleutians, some 300 miles west of Alaska's mainland. These are the Pribilof Islands, the northern hemisphere's "Galapagos Islands," a once-in-a-lifetime adventure.

Over 1.5 million Pacific Northern fur seals breed either on St. George or St. Paul islands.

A short stroll *above the shores of Lake Naknek are the cozy cabins of Brooks River Lodge. Moose antlers dotted along the path are a typically Alaskan decorative touch.*

These two islands and a few off-shore rocks support over 100 million birds—one of the most extraordinary displays of wildlife in the world.

A Russian discovery

During the era of Catherine the Great of Russia history-making Russian explorers were venturing farther and farther north from Siberia. They returned with conquests of new land for the Czarina and tales of incredible sights. Georg Wilhelm Steller brought word of magnificently furred water animals who swam the northern seas. He was referring to seals.

Later, returning seafarers told of seeing huge herds of fur seals swimming northward through the passes of the Aleutian Islands, then simply disappearing into the fog of the Bering Sea. These springtime sightings lent substance to the ancient Aleut legend of a mysterious group of islands far to the north of the Aleutian Chain where millions of fur seals gathered each year.

These misty, fog-bound islands were discovered by Russian explorer G. Pribylov in 1786. He had located the breeding grounds of the largest fur seal herd in the world. During the first year zealous hunters took some 40,000 seal skins, 2,000 sea otter skins, and 14,400 pounds of walrus ivory. The great fur rush was on. It proved to be the beginning of today's stormy international battle for conservation of one of the most beautiful and courageous animals known to man.

At one time, indiscriminate killing of seals for their valuable furs decimated the herds, but good management has rebuilt their population. The Pribilofs are home for sea otters, too, who also were once hunted almost to the point of extinction.

Getting to the Pribilofs

Three-day, two-night, or longer air excursions are offered from Anchorage via Cold Bay in the Aleutians to the island of St. Paul. The basic package includes air transportation, transfers, accommodations, and guided motor coach sightseeing to seal breeding grounds and bird rookeries.

You travel by Reeve Aleutian Airways; packages are put together by Alaska Tour & Marketing Services, Suite 312, Park Place Bldg., Seattle, WA 98101.

Food and lodging

Headquarters for all travelers is the Aleut-operated hotel on St. Paul—largest of the five Pribilof islands. Rooms in the town's hotel are simple and clean; bathrooms are "down the hall."

The dining room is a pleasant stroll away, located a few blocks down the main street of this small town. Everyone eats together. Menu selection is fairly limited, but the food is well cooked—and quite expensive. If you're planning a cocktail, bring your own. A small tavern next to the hotel serves beer and soft drinks.

Prices in the community store are about the best in Alaska. Souvenirs include native crafts and "Pribilof" sweatshirts.

The small Russian church in town is probably the most fascinating in Alaska. Built in the early part of the century, it has a traditional shape, but the onion dome is made of gold-painted metal, and the cross above the gate is constructed from sections of pipe. The interior of the church is one of the richest and most colorful in Alaska. Services are held Saturday evening and Sunday morning in Slavonic, Aleut, and English.

A brief Aleut history

The Pribilof Islands were uninhabited when discovered. Captive Aleuts were brought in to help kill and skin the seals.

Only the two largest islands (St. Paul and St. George) are occupied today by the local Aleut people. These Aleuts are descendants of those enslaved by early traders to harvest rich pelts from the abundant marine mammals.

Today, only some 3,000 Aleuts remain, 600 of whom live on St. Paul and St. George, giving these two villages the largest Aleut population in a single location in the entire world.

Most of the 450 Aleut people now living on St. Paul speak both Aleut and English fluently; many also use the Slavonic language effectively. During three months of the year, the seasonal fur seal harvest occupies most of the natives. During the rest of the year, the people exist mainly on welfare, supplementing their food with subsistence hunting of sea lions, birds, and reindeer.

A little about St. Paul

St. Paul Island is about 13½ miles long and 8 miles wide. It has roughly 45 miles of shoreline, composed of alternate stretches of sand and broken rock. Cliffs often rise as high as 400 feet above the water. No trees break the rolling, grassy plains that are covered with wildflowers in the summer.

From atop one of the cinder cones sprinkled around, you get a look at the village, several fresh-water lakes, and the small reindeer herd.

A story of birds and seals

Visitors come to the Pribilofs to see the bird and seal spectacle. Native guides in rickety buses

(Continued on page 97)

Tidy hillside village *is St. Paul,*
Aleut community in Pribilof Islands.

Alert blue fox kits *play in*
tall grass on St. Paul Island.

Preserving the wilderness

Statistics only hint at the size and grandeur of Alaska. Largest state in the union, Alaska spans four time zones, and boasts of our highest mountains, longest scenic rivers, more than half of our coastline, and most of our dwindling wildlife.

In contrast to the Lower 48, Alaska's lands appear virtually unmarked, affected only by seasons, weather, the descent of a glacier down a mountain valley, or the migration of a caribou herd across the tundra.

A current struggle between industry and conservationists holds Alaska's future in the balance. If the Alaska National Interest Lands Conservation Act passed Congress in its most generous form, nearly 40 percent of Alaska would be preserved.

Added to already existing parks and refuges would be such scenic splendors as Gates of the Arctic National Park, encompassing north and south slopes of the Brooks Range; Lake Clark National Park, spectacular meeting spot of the Alaska and Aleutian ranges; Kobuk Valley National Monument, Alaska's sandy Sahara; Wrangell - St. Elias National Park, the continent's greatest peaks and glaciers in one gigantic collection; Aniakchak Caldera National Monument, a spectacle of volcanism; Kenai Fjords National Park, a land of ice; Yukon-Charley National Rivers; and wildlife refuges for millions of birds, sea lions, seals, otters, walrus, whales, and polar bears.

Acreage would be added to Katmai National Monument, Mt. McKinley National Park, and Glacier Bay National Monument to preserve entire ecosystems. One grizzly bear needs 100 square miles just to feed itself and rear its young. Because the land is relatively unproductive and so fragile, parks and refuges must be larger than in the Lower 48.

Everyone agrees that some portion of this primeval wilderness should be preserved. The question is, how much? When Secretary William H. Seward engineered the purchase of Alaska from Russia in 1867, most people thought of this country as an "icebox." They never dreamed of its varied landscapes: lush rain forests, towering mountain ranges, rolling tundra plains, braided rivers, and islands and lakes too numerous to name.

Underneath the beauty, though, lie vast untapped resources of precious oil, gas, and minerals. Virtually unlimited forests attract lumbering interests. And the natives, visualizing the economic possibilities, want a share of this potential affluence.

The resulting Alaska Native Claims Settlement Act of 1971 not only gave the Eskimos, Aleuts, and Indians claim to 44 million acres but also added, as an afterthought, an amendment setting aside land for possible national parks, forests, wildlife refuges, and scenic and wild rivers.

Thus the controversy began between conservatives and developers. A federally protected wilderness would prohibit the haphazard industrialization that has so readily begun elsewhere. It appears likely that the wilderness proposition will include a compromise, though, allowing boats, aircraft, snowmobiles for subsistence hunting, and perhaps even roads in any new parks.

The urge to preserve Alaska's untouched wilderness clashes head-on with economic pressures. It's a large challenge for such a big land.

…Continued from page 94

bounce along the island's dirt roads, taking you to rookeries and good bird-sighting spots.

Warm, clear weather is rare. Bring warm, rainproof clothing and comfortable shoes for wet, windy weather.

The seals. It has never been established why the fur seal herd swims over 5,000 miles annually between southern California, northern Japan and the Pribilofs. But every other aspect of seal life is being carefully studied and recorded by scientists and biologists who come to the islands from all over the world.

Life in a harem. The vanguard of the great fur seal herd, the breeding bulls (or "beachmasters" as they are popularly known), reach the rookeries early in May. Here they take up their territory on well-defined beach areas smoothed by erosion and centuries of use by earlier generations of seals. These massive bulls are tremendously powerful animals, measuring 6 to 7 feet in length and weighing between 450 and 600 pounds—about five times as much as the females.

The bull must reach at least 7 years of age before he can acquire a harem; once he has collected his cows, he dares not leave even to eat or drink for fear of losing them. He sleeps very little and, during the breeding season, he is a vicious, restless, uncompromising lord and master over his "wives."

The battle for harems begins when the females arrive in June to give birth and breed again. A scene of wild confusion ensues—along with a cacophony of seal sounds.

A harem may include as many as 75 to 100 cows, but the average number is 30 to 40, generally the number assembled in one harem before a neighboring bull, a few feet away, has a chance to acquire one to start his own.

The unattached or idle bulls form a solid fringe outside the breeding rookeries, maintaining a constant vigil for a stray wife or two to start their own families. It's no wonder the beachmasters are in an exhausted, emaciated condition after the breeding season is over, sleeping for days before going to sea for food.

Each breeding cow bears one pup a year. After their arrival on the islands, the cows give birth within a few days. The pups weigh between 10 and 12 pounds at birth. As the young grow stronger, they wander over the rookery gathering in groups (called pods) while their mothers swim to feeding grounds some 250 miles away. The females have an uncanny instinct for recognizing their own young and will nurse no other.

Harems begin breaking up in early August; the herd leaves the islands as gradually as it arrived, an earnest exodus beginning in October and reaching a peak in November. By the end of the year, the snow-covered beaches are usually deserted.

Singly and in small groups, the fur seals make their way through the passes of the Aleutian Islands to seek food and warmer climates until the time comes to return for their annual rendezvous on the mist-shrouded Pribilofs.

Viewing the spectacle. Because seals are easily disturbed by humans who approach too closely, blinds with peepholes have been erected. Behind these you observe the antics without inhibiting the seals. Bring binoculars for a close look.

Fur harvesting of bachelor bulls starts the latter part of June; movies of the event are shown at the hotel in the evening. If you are there during harvesting and have a stout stomach, you can watch the ancient ritual of rounding up and clubbing. All visitors are invited to take a look at the processing plant where pelts are treated and packed for shipping.

The birds. Even if you were not a bird watcher before you arrived, you'll end up comparing notes with other members of your group on what exotic birds were sighted or photographed.

These islands are an ornithological paradise —one of the largest bird sanctuaries in the world. Over 180 species can be sighted, some extremely rare, like the Mongolian wheatear. Asiatic species often wander into these islands. This is also virtually the only place in the world to sight the red-legged kittiwake.

Shaggy and gentle, *musk oxen are a Pleistocene remnant. On Nunivak Island they are raised for their cashmere-soft wool, called qiviut.*

Behind *blind, visitors watch fur seals on rocks below. Passing Coast Guard ship patrols waters.*

Wriggling mass *of seals mate and breed on Pribilof beaches in late June, early July.*

The island is also one of the few places where other species may be seen in such large numbers. Hundreds of bird rookeries dot the beaches and cliffs of St. Paul, and there is no rarer treat than watching these beautiful and capricious creatures in their natural habitat.

A list of the Pribilof Island birds, which visitors can pick up on arrival at the hotel, helps you to get started at bird watching. You'll also find that a bird identification book comes in handy. Be sure to take along your camera (with telephoto lens) or you'll miss a good shot.

Brilliantly colored flowers, ferns, and foliage make the island a horticulturist's heaven—as well as a good hideaway for many a small bird. Some people enjoy tramping through the lush, grassy terrain and along the rocky cliffs to record a shore or sea bird. Others find a comfortable viewing spot on the tundra and don't budge from it. Either approach can lead to remarkable success.

Guides give tips in locating birds and know their scientific names and nesting habits. Binoculars aid viewing.

The mainland town of Bethel

Bethel, near the mouth of the Kuskokwim River, is the main community along the southwestern mainland. The surrounding area contains a number of wildlife refuges for nesting waterfowl and shore birds.

A supply center for the vast delta of the Kuskokwim River, Bethel makes a convenient jumping-off spot for visiting many outlying native villages by boat or air charter.

A visit to Bethel shows still another face of Alaska. Here the flat, virtually treeless tundra, divided only by rivers, stretches to the horizon.

Bethel is the principal town on Alaska's second largest river, the Kuskokwim. Important to the livelihood of this region, the Kuskokwim provides fish and serves as a water highway between villages.

Originally an Eskimo village and trading post, Bethel is now a supply center for many neighboring bush villages.

Commercial fishing is part of the town's economic base, as is the outfitting and guiding of hunters. Residents and visitors enjoy sportfishing for sheefish, salmon, and northern pike in the river, as well as angling for trout in nearby lakes. Game in the region includes moose, wolf, beaver, muskrat, and various waterfowl.

As you walk around town you are likely to see salmon or caribou skins drying on racks outside homes. At Yugtarvik (formerly the Bethel Museum) you'll find a collection of Eskimo artifacts and arts and crafts for sale, including the delicate handwoven baskets from the Yukon and Kuskokwim deltas.

The modern, 75-room Kuskokwim Hotel with dining room and conference and banquet facilities comes as a surprise in such a remote spot. Several local restaurants offer traditional menus.

Bethel can be reached year-round on Wien Air Alaska from Anchorage. A number of air taxi services in Bethel offer flightseeing tours to outlying villages.

Trips from Bethel

By plane or riverboat, a visitor can reach out-of-the-way villages unknown to many tourists. Here you can experience a face of Alaska totally different from more developed areas.

The Clarence Rhode National Wildlife Refuge, north of Bethel on the Norton Sound, encompasses some 2.8 million acres of some of the greatest waterfowl breeding grounds in the world. Waters of more than 50,000 lakes, combined with low delta coastline and offshore islands, provide vast nesting grounds in a tundra environment.

Birds such as black brant, Arctic loon, emperor and snow goose, as well as ducks, gulls, and land birds, populate the refuge in unbelievable numbers.

Unalakleet, on Norton Sound, north of the mouth of the Unalakleet River, is located in a hilly area covered by spruce trees.

Unalakleet has a hotel and coffee shop, also a lighted runway allowing regular jet service. An Air Force installation 8 miles away provides jobs for many villagers. To add to their livelihood, natives also fish and trap during the season.

The village serves as a take-off point for sport fishing in the area and on the Unalakleet River.

Out to Nunivak Island

One popular excursion from Bethel is a flight to the native village of Mekoryuk on Nunivak Island, 160 air miles to the west. Mekoryuk, once an Eskimo village, today thrives upon a reindeer meat-processing plant—the economic core of the town.

Nunivak Island is one of the few areas in the world where the shaggy musk ox roams free. These gentle beasts are cultivated for their *qiviut,* the cashmere-soft wool used in knitting garments.

Some of the finest ivory carving in the world is done here. Villagers also make unique wooden masks. Accommodations for tourists are quite limited and you'll need to make advance arrangements before planning an overnight stay.

Feathers and furs: wildlife of Alaska

Alaska offers a bonanza of birds and wildlife for visitor viewing. You'll find birds, sea mammals, and big game animals from the southeastern tip of the Panhandle to the farthest point of the frozen Arctic coast.

Listed below are some of the most plentiful of the numerous birds and animals in the state and the areas where they can be found.

Birds

More species of birds are found in Alaska than in any other state. Even in the chilliest reaches of the Arctic, birdlife abounds.

The Pribilof Islands are an ornithological paradise, playing host to some 180 species of birds.

The bald eagle, a most conspicuous bird, is found in greater numbers in Alaska than in all the other states combined. Prime habitat for bald eagles is the forested coastline and offshore islands of Southeast Alaska. One of the heaviest concentrations dwells on the 678-mile coastline of Admiralty Island, where the average is almost two nests per mile. The Chilkat Valley near Haines is another favorite nesting area.

Eagles nest solitarily atop spiring snags, returning to the same nest year after year. The white headfeathers of the mature eagle gave this regal bird its name (the term "bald" was commonly used during the 17th and 18th centuries to signify white). Immature birds are completely brown.

Grouse and ptarmigan come in several different kinds and species in Alaska. It takes a sharp eye to spot the well-camouflaged ptarmigan, Alaska's state bird. In summer its subtle color blends with the brown of the tundra. As the year advances it takes on the snowy white of its wintry background.

Of all the grouse in Alaska, the spruce grouse seems most at home. These birds eat the needles of the spruce trees almost all year.

You'll find handsome blue grouse in Southeast Alaska and small ptarmigan in the Arctic. These birds never fail to tempt the hunter and photographer alike.

Shore birds in Alaska are another fascination for those who learn when and where to look for them. The coastal waters from Ketchikan to the Pribilof Islands abound with seafaring murres, murrelets, puffins, cormorants, and gulls.

Some of the "bird cliffs" harbor thousands of nesting sea birds, incubating their eggs in most unlikely nooks and crannies.

Inland species found in marshy river bottoms include ducks, swans, and geese. An international flavor in birdlife occurs when the wheatears arrive from Asia, the golden plovers fly in from Hawaii, and the warblers come north from Mexico and South America.

Even in winter a surprising variety of seasonal residents arrive: chickadees, jays, woodpeckers, several kinds of owl, water ouzels, and ubiquitous ravens.

Sea mammals

Seals, sea lions, whales, and porpoises are prominent in Alaskan waters. The most uncommon ribbon seal is found in the northwestern Bering Sea and along the coast from Pt. Barrow to the Aleutians. Harbor seals also inhabit Alaskan waters from the northern Bering Sea down through Southeast Alaska. Ringed seals are found only in the far northern waters.

The large bearded seals, weighing up to 700 pounds, are found in the Bering, Chukchi, and Arctic waters. They are characterized by pronounced facial whiskers.

Fur seals usually spend most of their time in the open ocean, hauling themselves out on the Pribilof Islands in late spring. The Gulf of Alaska and waters to the south form the territory of the Steller sea lions, large relatives of the fur seal. Good seal-watching spots are located along Ketchikan's waterfront and along the highway north of Juneau.

Many whales and porpoises are seen by visitors to Alaska. The most prominent of the big whales is the humpbacked. Difficult to identify in the water, it often obliges by jumping right out into view. Killer whales have long dorsal fins and striking white markings. The Beluga whales of Cook Inlet and the Bering Sea are completely white. After whales, porpoises look surprisingly small. Harbor porpoises are gray; Dall's porpoises have white areas on their backs. You'll chance upon them anywhere from the Panhandle northward.

Sea otters, portly members of the weasel family, usually float on their backs, their heads and feet just visible above the water. They inhabit shallow areas of the coastline.

The toothy walrus never ventures south of the Bering Sea. He migrates north in spring to the Chukchi Sea, following closely behind the ice breakup.

Big game animals

A sportsman's and photographer's paradise, Alaska has as many big game animals as the rest of the United States put together. Somewhere along your trip you'll get at least a glimpse of a few of these impressive creatures.

Bears come in several sizes and colors. Black bears are found all over the state. They are also called "glacier bears" in the Glacier Bay area of Southeast Alaska, and "cinnamon bears" elsewhere.

The larger brown bear is found throughout the state's southern coastal area—from the Panhandle to the Alaska Peninsula, as well as on Kodiak Island.

Its near relative, the grizzly, ranges in color from light blonde to black. Visitors usually view the blonde version of the grizzly bear from a distance at Mt. McKinley National Park.

Polar bears, the northern relative, inhabit the Bering Sea and Arctic Ocean ice packs. This shy white creature is protected against hunters.

Bison were introduced to Alaska in the early 1900s. A large herd now roams the Big Delta region south of Fairbanks, sometimes wandering so close to the Alaska Highway that motorists have to be alert to avoid them.

Caribou wander in herds across the interior and northern parts of the state. One of the likeliest places to see these nomadic creatures is Mt. McKinley National Park.

Curly-horned Dall sheep make their home in all of Alaska's major mountains. At Sheep Mountain, a reserve along the highway northeast of Anchorage, travelers can watch the sheep high up on the mountainsides. They can also be seen in Mt. McKinley Park.

Elk are barely accessible in Alaska. Both large herds are on islands: Afognak and Raspberry islands near Kodiak, and Revillagigedo Island near Ketchikan.

Moose are common sights throughout Alaska. This large, ungainly member of the deer family wanders in great numbers long the highway between Anchorage and Fairbanks. On the Kenai Peninsula, there is a range of natural wilderness set aside for them.

Musk oxen, native to Alaska, became extinct in the mid-1800s. Early in this century, a few of these shaggy beasts were brought over from Greenland and placed on Nunivak Island. Now a thriving herd, they are rarely seen by visitors. Their cashmere-like fleece is used to knit fine gift items sold in major city shops.

Sitka deer have a characteristic black tail. In spring and early summer, they sometimes approach southeastern roadways early in the morning or late in the evening. They are also found in the Prince William Sound area and on Kodiak Island.

Alaskan wolves are very wary. You may hear them calling, but it's doubtful that you'll see them. Mt. McKinley Park provides your best chance. Many have retreated into the Arctic regions, following the caribou herds.

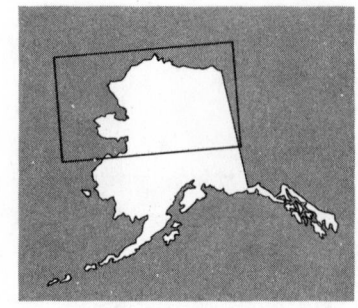

The Far North

Visitors to Arctic Alaska have an opportunity to enjoy one of the most unusual regions of the United States. A fascinating land, the Arctic adds high adventure to any northern trip.

Regularly scheduled flights reach the Arctic's few large cities; bush pilots make runs to more remote sections of "Eskimoland." Comfortable, though not necessarily luxurious, hotels await guests. Accommodations are gradually being expanded to handle an increasing number of visitors.

Alaska's 200,000-square-mile Arctic comprises the northern third of the state. Though much of it is vast rolling country, it also contains surprising mountains, such as the Brooks Range. Its scant population of a little more than 17,000 could be lost in Pasadena's Rose Bowl.

During winter a continuous icy sheet weds land and sea, melting only in late spring. Temperatures remain low in winter, but much of the land receives no more precipitation than Phoenix, Arizona. The snow that falls remains permanently frozen on the ground.

Permafrost may be only a few feet deep in some places; in others, it reaches down several thousand feet. It is covered by a treeless mat known as tundra—a layer of springy mosses, sedges, and dwarf willow and spruce.

In summer, the offshore ice melts, permitting ocean-going vessels to pass. On land, a bright carpet of wildflowers flares into brief bloom; summer temperatures soar up to 70°.

At Point Barrow, the sun does not set from May 11 to August 2; in Kotzebue, the sun is above the horizon for 36 days between June 3 and July 9. The late spring visitor may have the thrill of seeing the ice "go out" (usually between June 5 and 15) or of spotting a polar bear from the air.

In dollars and cents terms, the Arctic's economy is based on tourism and exploration for natural resources. The North Slope oil discoveries stimulated accelerating industrializa-tion here where the military Distant Early Warning Line is strung out along the top of the world.

Even though their age-old fishing and hunting economy is rapidly changing, some of the sturdy Eskimos cling to that way of life. There are still old traders and a sprinkling of trappers. Excitement runs high during whaling and hunting seasons; fish are an important food staple. Women make beautiful fur garments, following patterns of their ancestors; men carve ivory from walrus tusks into figurines and jewelry.

How to get there

The only way average visitors can reach the land of the Eskimos is by air. A network of scheduled and bush routes reaches into nearly 100 scattered villages. In many places snowmobiles have replaced dog teams during the winter for local transportation.

Travelers who cross the Arctic Circle on any of the air tours receive impressive certificates stating they've been to the Far North. In this land of aurora borealis and midnight sun, a visitor can fly in continuous daylight.

Arctic gateway cities are Anchorage and Fairbanks. In addition to scheduled jet service on Alaska Airlines and Wien Air Alaska, air taxi operators provide service to practically any point in this region.

Reduced-cost air fares are available to Nome, Kotzebue, Barrow, and Prudhoe Bay from both

In Kotzebue's *Living Museum of the Arctic, Eskimo dancers perform before animal exhibit.*

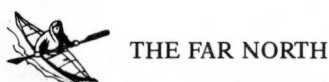

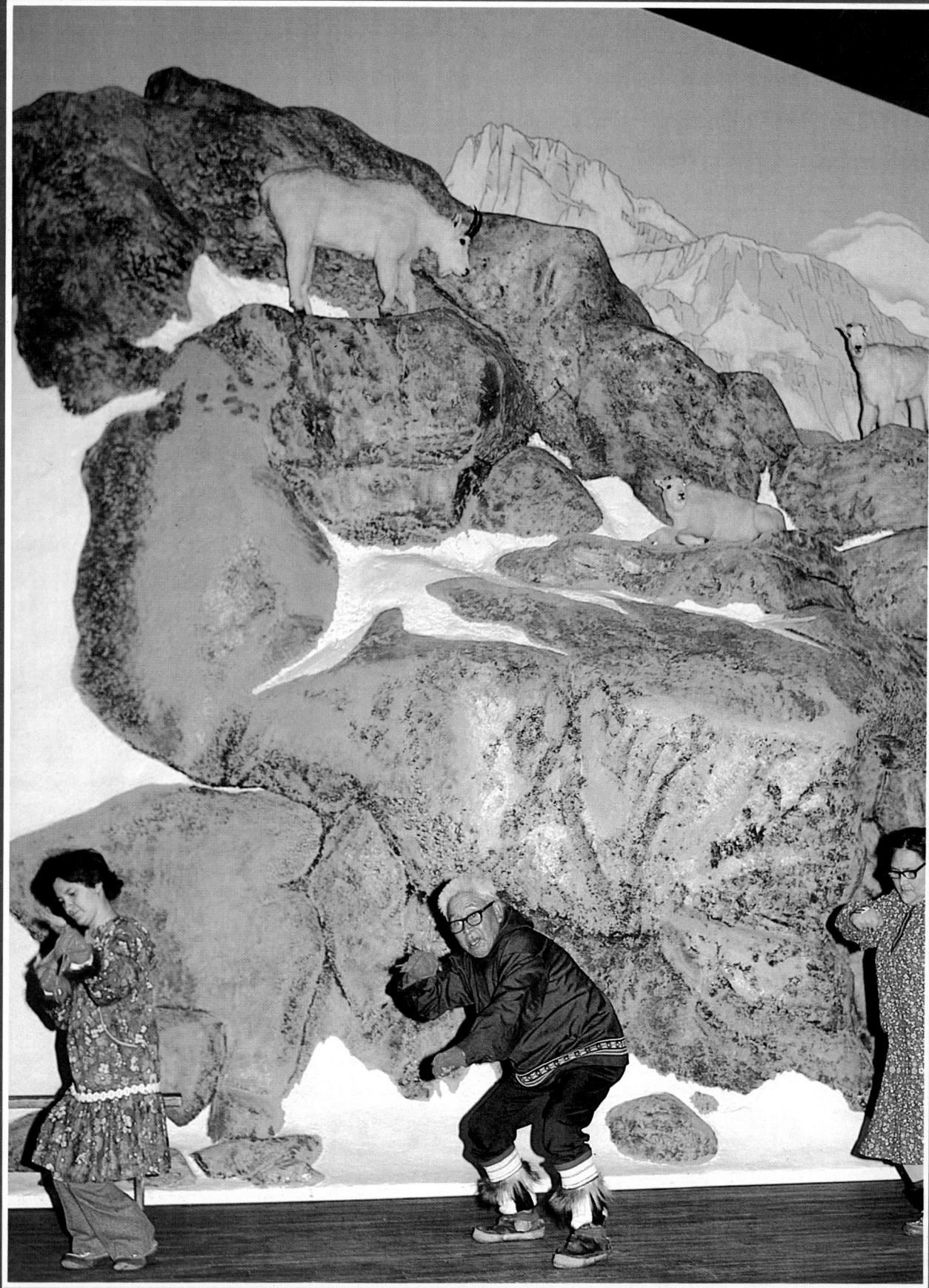

The Arctic

Barrow—top of the continent

Blanket tosses
Eskimo dancing
Naval Arctic Research Laboratory
Rogers & Post monument
Tundra tour

Fort Yukon—Athabascan Indian village
features beadwork, fish, and furs

Kotzebue—colorful Eskimo village

Dog sled ride
Jade factory
Living Museum of the Arctic
Ootukakuktuvik Museum
Reindeer camp

Nome—former gold camp

Gold panning
King Island Eskimo Dancers
Museums

Prudhoe Bay—pipeline terminus

Birdwatching
Community center tour
Geological film

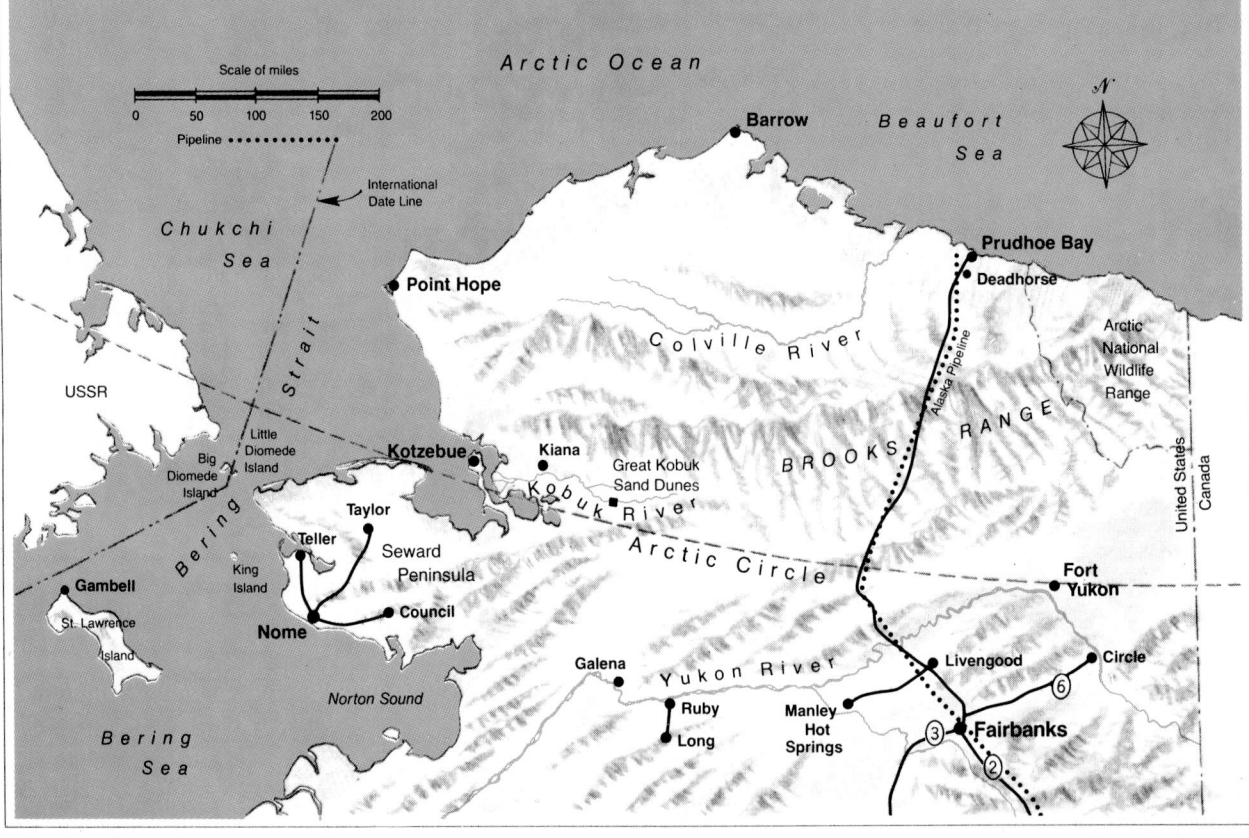

Anchorage and Fairbanks, providing you have booked a package itinerary. Consult your travel agent for information.

What to wear

Despite high temperatures in summer, you should bring a warm sweater and comfortable walking shoes. For a winter trip, wear thermal underwear, boots, mittens or gloves, a hat, and a woolen or down coat. Guided tours to the seacoast cities of Nome, Kotzebue, and Barrow provide guests with colorful, Eskimo-style parkas to wear while there.

Nome was a gold town

Spawned by discovery of gold on the beaches in 1898, Nome boomed into a gold rush camp of tents and frame buildings. It once boasted 40,000 residents. Today, Eskimos constitute about 70 percent of Nome's population of 2,500.

Although the gold rush has passed with the decline of mining, an aura of the glamorous days lingers on. Today's city is a far cry from the tent community of years ago, but you will see reminders of that bygone era. The romance, sudden fortunes, and crooked politicians of Nome's early days inspired Rex Beach to write *The Spoilers*.

Considered a part of the Arctic, Nome is technically 30 miles south of the Arctic Circle. Its appearance is deceptively drab. You'll have to look indoors for the local color. Houses and business buildings lean unevenly, reflecting their footing on permafrost. Some are kept level with house jacks; others are mounted on skids ready to be moved when the permafrost melts.

Several modern structures, including hotels, museums, and gift shops, stand on the west side of the main street—the only strip of land that is not permafrost. A massive breakwater shields them from the fury of winter storms.

Highlights

Most package tours include both Nome and Kotzebue, with an overnight in one town or the other. Nome has a number of hotels (including three Nugget Inns), dining rooms, cocktail lounges, and a good bakery.

During the summer season, daily sightseeing trips with driver-guides are offered. It may be a surprise to find more than 300 varieties of wildflowers on the Seward Peninsula, carpeting the ground you walk.

The tour visits abandoned gold mining areas and gives you a look at a working mine. An old-timer will show you how to wield a gold pan in the hope that you may get some "color."

Photographing wildlife

A camera and one or more telephoto lenses will enrich your visit to Mt. McKinley. No other park in North America offers a similar opportunity to photograph such a variety of wildlife.

A 35 mm, single-lens reflex camera is perhaps the most useful tool for wildlife portraits. A standard lens, medium telephoto lens, and long telephoto lens will provide a suitable range.

For animal studies, a 200 mm lens is perhaps the most useful. It brings images close, can be hand-held, and is lightweight enough to carry easily.

Tele-converters are inexpensive attachments designed to double the focal length of any lens. Their disadvantage is that they reduce the amount of light allowed into the camera lens by one or more stops to adjust for the converter. Follow the directions that accompany the converter.

Variable focal-length zoom lenses are easy to use and practical for wildlife photography. But experts consider them not as critically sharp as fixed focal-length lenses.

Although not as quick and easy to use as a 35 mm camera, a larger single-lens reflex camera is also suitable for wildlife photography. On the whole, twin-lens reflex and range-finder cameras are slower to use.

Eskimo boy *warms up on caribou skin before classic high toss.*

Nome's parka-clad visitors *get pointers on Arctic gold panning.*

The King Island Eskimo Dancers perform for groups. These master ivory carvers long ago traveled 80 miles in walrus-hide boats to reach Nome from their earlier home in the Bering Sea.

Several gift shops are attached to museums. They feature examples of native craftsmenship, especially carved walrus ivory and soapstone. Fine furs, mukluks, and parkas are also sold. Nome is the best place in the Arctic to buy gold nugget and jade jewelry.

Since Nome is the aerial center for this part of Alaska, you can make arrangements to take bush trips with mail pilots to more remote Eskimo villages, such as Unalakleet, Shishmaref, Wales, Teller, Little Diomede Island (2½ miles from Siberian Big Diomede Island), and Golovin.

Side trip to Gambell

One of the Arctic villages travelers can visit is Gambell, on St. Lawrence Island within sight of Siberia's Chukotsky Peninsula. Until recently this small society of Eskimo hunters and fishermen had little contact with the outside world. Archaelogical evidence indicates the island was inhabited 2,400 years ago.

It's a friendly community. You will see villagers curing hides and meat, foraging the tundra fields for bird eggs and bitter berries, or setting out in their skin boats to hunt walrus, whale, seal, and sea lion. Life on the ocean is serious and basic for Gambell residents. But many lives have been saved from the unfriendly sea by one modern device—the outboard motor.

Bird watchers will particularly enjoy exploring Gambell Mountain, the rolling tundra fields, and beaches near the village. Arctic terns, gulls, sea parrots, auklets, jaegers, murres, puffins, and cormorants are just a few of St. Lawrence Island's summer residents.

Special events

A March visitor to Nome will find that modern, motorized racing machines have replaced many of the early dog sled teams. Excitement prevails in the annual Nome-Teller-Nome Snow Machine Classic, covering about 140 miles round trip.

Nome marks the end of the 1,000-mile-long Iditarod Sled Dog Race trail that begins in Anchorage. In March, Nome's residents greet contestants as they cross the finish line.

A major annual event is the Midnight Sun Festival in June. Highlights include a midnight sun baseball game, foot races, and raft races on the Nome River. Oldtimers and newcomers dress in costumes to celebrate continuous daylight.

The Fourth of July is always an old-fashioned celebration in most towns in the Arctic. All these events present photographic opportunities.

Kotzebue: a modern Eskimo village

Named for Otto von Kotzebue, a navigator who discovered the village in 1816, this rapidly growing Eskimo settlement thrives 30 miles north of the Arctic Circle. The air route to it from Nome passes within 150 miles of East Cape, Siberia.

On June 3 the sun is above the horizon, where it remains, swinging in a great circle in the sky, for the following 36 days. One of the great photo subjects during this period is the midnight sun; shoot it at 20-minute intervals as it dips toward the northern horizon and rises again without ever going out of sight. At the Nul-Luk-Vik Hotel, a second-floor observation lounge makes it easy to watch this phenomenon.

In mid-June, by ice break, the ice flows from the rivers for about two weeks. You'll see small children with oars using floes for boats.

Kotzebue has no sidewalks. The colorful main street runs along the beach. Here you'll find the modern Nu-Luk-Vik Hotel. The hotel has a second story restaurant and lounge where summer visitors watch the midnight sun. Other streets ramble between buildings without any pattern. Standing well north of timberline, Kotzebue boasts only one tree, a dubious specimen that is nevertheless proudly pointed out to visitors.

The natives live with one foot in the modern era and the other in their old way of life. Though they'll eat corn flakes, they prefer muktuk, the outer skin of whale.

After the ice goes out, the beluga (white) whales migrate. Much excitement is generated as the whalers put out to sea for these highly-prized animals, which attain 12 to 17 feet in length and average about 100 pounds to the foot. During June and July, you may see these whales being cut up, their meat hung on racks along the street to dry for winter food.

Boats manned by modern Eskimos are similar in style to those made by their ancestors, but in most cases materials have changed. The familiar kayak, and the oomiak, an oval-shaped vessel originally made of walrus skin, are still used.

Wooden prefab houses have virtually replaced traditional sod and driftwood dwellings in all but the most remote areas. In many yards, dogs are chained to houses. Though these dogs may look docile, they're usually unfriendly to strangers, so don't venture too close.

Highlights

For a quick once-over, it's smart to take a sightseeing tour with a guide. Outfitted with colorful Eskimo parkas, visitors are driven to such local attractions as old village sites, an authentic sod igloo, and a jade factory.

Tourists can ride on a dog sled (with rubber tires) and watch Eskimo dances done to chants and the beat of native-made skin drums. These dances tell stories of the hunt and other activities vital to the lives of the Eskimo people. Blanket-tossing in a walrus skin is another popular activity.

Kotzebue has two museums: the Living Museum of the Arctic, constructed in 1976, where dramatic, lifelike dioramas depict and interpret Eskimo history and culture as well as Arctic environment and wildlife; and Ootukakuktuvik (an Eskimo word meaning "place of old things"), featuring an excellent collection of Eskimo arts and crafts.

A few shops offer excellent ivory and soapstone carvings and interesting jade jewelry.

By extending your stay, you can take a bush pilot tour to many small Eskimo villages seldom seen by visitors, or make a trip to the Jade Mountain area, where you might find your own jade nugget.

The Kobuk River country, probably the Arctic's most scenic area, contains a dozen or so Eskimo villages. Kiana is one of the more modern; there is a lodge where you can stay overnight. Nearby is a unique geological feature, the Kobuk Sand Dunes—about 25 square miles of Sahara Desert, incredible as it may seem in the Arctic.

Sheefishing is popular at Kiana. The sheefish, unique to Alaska, is a good fighting fish not known to many anglers. You can sample it at the hotel restaurant in Kotzebue.

Side trip to Point Hope

Point Hope is a truly remote Eskimo village where you get the feeling of the real, rugged, timeless, isolated—yet friendly—Arctic. Its residents own hundreds of handsome sled dogs.

Called Tigara (index finger), this village has been continually occupied for more than 1,000 years because of its profitable whaling and hunting. In 1826, the British explorer Capt. F. W. Beechey named the 12-mile-long sandspit for Sir William Johnstone. Erosion by the sea threatened the village with relocation. A new village has been built. The old one is still intact, but most villagers have moved to the new site.

As a tour destination, Point Hope is a real adventure—but it's not for everyone. Limited overnight accommodations (for 8 persons) are surprisingly clean and comfortable. Cooking facilities (with utensils and dishes) and two local stores where you can buy food make it possible to fix your own meals. It's also possible to eat at local coffee shops.

On a guided walking tour, you visit the old sod igloo village, underground natural deep-freeze

meat storage, whale-feasting grounds, mission church, cemetery completely fenced with whale jaw bones, as well as an occupied sod igloo home where you will be shown how to operate the seal oil lamp.

Special events

The Fourth of July always calls for a big festival of Eskimo dancing, kayak racing, Eskimo high jumping, muktuk-eating contest, choosing of a queen, and many interesting and strictly Eskimo games.

Barrow – northernmost U.S. city

Sir John Barrow's name is preserved at Point Barrow—northernmost point in the United States. This man helped finance many polar expeditions, including that of Franklin and Parry.

The settlement of Barrow, with a population of over 2,500, is the largest Eskimo village in the world. Barrow's most famous resident was Charlie Brower, who wrote *50 Years Before Zero*. Many of his descendants still live in the village.

American whalers followed the big bowhead whale into the Arctic Ocean after the 1870s. Whaling is still an important activity for the Eskimos. If the hunts are successful in early spring, a colorful whale feast and celebration is held in June or July.

Point Barrow came into the news when Will Rogers and Wiley Post crashed near there in 1935 during an around-the-world flight. A Rogers-Post Monument is located 12 miles southwest of the village. The airfield near the village has been named the Rogers-Post Airport.

Barrow probably has the starkest appearance of any city in the Arctic. Much of the year the Arctic Ocean is frozen solid from Barrow to the North Pole, 1,200 miles away.

The jerry-built village is randomly clustered along a barren strand of beach fronting the Arctic Ocean. There are no sidewalks, no water or sewer systems. Water must be transported from a small lake 4 miles inland; during winter, drinking water is melted ice. The city starts "spring housecleaning" by mid-June, probably the best time to visit.

The modern Top of the World Hotel will surprise you; it has 40 rooms, gift shop, coffee shop, and restaurant. Browerville, a suburb, has a restaurant with local delicacies. In town, hot doughnuts are the bakery specialty.

Four miles north of Barrow, the Naval Arctic Research Laboratory contains a museum featuring native handicrafts and scientific specimens. The facility is open only to group tours.

Both bus and walking tours are conducted by

knowledgeable guides. You will watch Eskimo dances (join in if you feel so inclined) and blanket tossing. Following the festivities, a "flea market" of local handicrafts is held. You bargain directly with the Eskimos.

Brooks Range, *appearing deceptively lofty, juts out of the otherwise flat Arctic tundra.*

If you're curious, you can dig down to permafrost—the frozen subsoil that never thaws. In summer, even though the top layer of earth is tufted with wildflowers and grasses, the ground is still frozen underneath.

Beginning of a pipeline

Deadhorse is where you land when you spend a day at Prudhoe Bay, northern terminus of the Alaska pipeline. The locale around town looks something like an enclave out of science fiction. Crews live in movable trailers, comfortably heated, with community showers and dining areas.

If you're lucky, you'll be met by a driver-guide who is a geology major with a minor in ornithology. Various structures devoted to oil and birds are about all there is to see.

Your first stop is for a lunch with the workers. The price for this cafeteria meal is high, but you get coffee, fruit, and ice cream free.

A haul road from Fairbanks brings in heavy equipment; barges head out to the Beaufort Sea to pick up additional supplies. Huge tractors can move over the fragile tundra without leaving a mark.

The crews work in brutal weather to bring oil from deep below the 2,000-foot permafrost and

The sign *is a good-natured joke referring to the treeless setting of Prudhoe Bay—where only oil tanks and other industrial structures break the horizon.*

send it down the 4-foot pipe to the Gulf of Alaska. It's not surprising that their rest and recreation centers are so sumptuous.

At the "BP Hilton," a large community center, live trees grow up several stories and geraniums in planters brighten exercise areas and croquet courts. For entertainment, there are swimming pools, saunas, game rooms, and television tapes.

But the main attraction is the pipeline, snaking its way over the tundra, across mountains and rivers never conquered until now, to waiting boats in Valdez harbor. Environmentalists succeeded in attaining more careful treatment of the tundra and crossings for caribou herds along the pipeline's route.

Although Prudhoe Bay is not a particularly attractive destination, it does give you an interesting insight into the gargantuan task of laying the pipeline. Remember, though, that the tour to Deadhorse is an all-day bus trip though special overnight accommodations are offered visitors.

Fort Yukon is home for the Athabascans

Starting above Whitehorse in the Canadian Yukon, the great Yukon River flows in an arc of

Specially designed *for Prudhoe Bay, truck with doughnut tires can navigate frozen or slushy terrain— even water. Rumor says it can roll over a man without hurting him (but not all the evidence is in yet).*

2,081 miles to reach the Bering Sea. At the northernmost bend, above the Arctic Circle, it widens out to 3 miles. Here is the location of Fort Yukon, the largest Athabascan Indian village in Alaska.

Fort Yukon was the first English-speaking settlement. Established in 1847 as a fur trading post by the Hudson's Bay Company, it operated for 20 years. By 1873 the first gold prospectors had arrived.

Now the Yukon River is gradually eroding the old townsite, and new log cabins are being built on higher ground among the lean spruce trees. But the village hasn't changed a great deal over the years. Trading posts still do business in furs, thimbles, tractors, and general merchandise. Modern buildings contrast sharply with the primitive life style.

How to get there

Transportation has drastically changed. Instead of great sternwheel river steamers and barges that once plied between St. Michaels (near the Yukon river mouth) and Dawson, traffic today moves by air.

Air North has scheduled flights from Fairbanks to Fort Yukon; other air charter services offer half-day to one-day tours.

Where to stay

Fort Yukon Lodge is a large, two-story, log structure with nine rooms, kitchen, dining room, and expansive lobby with a huge wood-burning stove.

What to see and do

Athabascan Indian women tan moose and caribou hides and do exceptionally artistic beadwork. Beadwork moccasins and raw furs are good buys. Look for outstanding examples of Indian beadwork in the altar cloths of the log Episcopal Church. (The church's hymn books are printed in the Athabascan language.)

Along the river you will see fish wheels, ingenious devices with wire baskets powered by the river current. These baskets scoop up migrating salmon as they swim upstream. You can watch the natives cleaning and hanging up the fish which, after it dries, will provide winter food both for themselves and for their malemute dogs.

An additional attraction is a reconstruction of old Fort Yukon built from the original Hudson's Bay Company plans. The 1847-style fort includes a stockade, trading post, and small museum offering beadwork for sale.

Look up *to find the aristocratic Dall sheep. Their home is high among crags and mountain slopes.*

Caribou *gather on snow patch to seek relief from summer mosquitoes, warble flies.*

Index

Photographers

ATMS photo by Bob Giersdorf: 16, 31 top, 34, 42 left, 95 bottom, 103. **Captain Gregory Avdelas:** 23. **Sally Bishop:** 39 bottom, 42 right. **Barbara J. Braasch:** 13, 26 bottom, 31 bottom, 39 top, 44, 51, 57, 62 bottom, 65 bottom, 73 bottom, 87, 93, 95 top, 98, 106 top, 109 bottom. **Glenn M. Christiansen:** 4, 9, 26 top, 37, 40, 65 top, 84, 85. **Columbia Glacier Cruises:** 75. **Ed Cooper:** 47, 80 bottom. **Phyllis Elving:** 73 top. **Ken Erickson:** 10, 12, 33. **Robert Ewell:** 59 top. **Peter Henschel:** 109 top. **George Herben:** 111 bottom. **G. C. Kelley:** 18. **William S. Kimball:** 90. **Rick McIntyre:** 59 bottom. **Proctor Mellquist:** 61, 110. **Don Normark:** 1, 8, 97, back cover. **Willis Peterson:** 111 top. **Jeff Phillips:** 21, 29, 77, 80 top. **Alice Puster:** 70 bottom. **Dick Rowan:** 62 top. **Nancy Simmerman:** 78. **Harald Sund:** 54, 70 top, 82. **Tim Thompson:** 106 bottom. **Westours:** 67.